MANAGING THE KNOWLEDGE-INTENSIVE FIRM

Over the last decade, there has been a substantial rise in the number of knowledge-intensive firms – constituted primarily of professionals. The core assets of these businesses are the people themselves. Handle them badly, and they may defect or stall. Successful managers of knowledge-intensive firms must create meaning among and inspire their employees to ensure high performance. To achieve this, leaders must understand how to target each employee's ambitions and challenges to facilitate their personal and professional development.

This book examines what sets knowledge-intensive firms apart from other types of organizations, and the resultant organizational and strategic differences in business models, talent management, and client-handling approaches. The authors bring their own complementary perspectives on the subject: one, as the manager of a private consulting firm with a strong research background; another, as a business school professor whose practice-based skills are fundamental to his work; and a third, a world-leading commentator on professional service firms acting as a consultant, business school researcher, and a manager.

Ejler, Poulfelt and Czerniawska present a new model for transforming the management of knowledge-intensive firms, which is supported throughout with practical examples and cases.

Nicolaj Ejler is Director at Rambøll Management Consulting, Denmark.

Flemming Poulfelt is Professor of Management and Strategy and Vice-Dean at Copenhagen Business School, Denmark.

Fiona Czerniawska is Joint Managing Director and co-founder of Source Information Services Ltd, UK.

MANAGING THE KNOWLEDGE-INTENSIVE FIRM

Nicolaj Ejler, Flemming Poulfelt and Fiona Czerniawska

LONDON AND NEW YORK

First published 2011
by Routledge
2 Park Square, Milton Park, Abingdon, Oxon, OX14 4RN

Simultaneously published in the USA and Canada
by Routledge
711 Third Avenue, New York, NY10017

Routledge is an imprint of the Taylor & Francis Group, an informa business

© 2011 Nicolaj Ejler, Flemming Poulfelt and Fiona Czerniawska

The right of Nicolaj Ejler, Flemming Poulfelt and Fiona Czerniawska to be identified as authors of this work has been asserted by them in accordance with sections 77 and 78 of the Copyright, Designs and Patents Act 1988.

All rights reserved. No part of this book may be reprinted or reproduced or utilised in any form or by any electronic, mechanical, or other means, now known or hereafter invented, including photocopying and recording, or in any information storage or retrieval system, without permission in writing from the publishers.

Trademark notice: Product or corporate names may be trademarks or registered trademarks, and are used only for identification and explanation without intent to infringe.

British Library Cataloguing in Publication Data
A catalogue record for this book is available from the British Library

Library of Congress Cataloguing in Publication Data
Ejler, Nicolaj
Managing the knowledge intensive firm/Nicolaj Ejler, Flemming Poulfelt and Fiona Czerniawska. -- 1st ed.
p. cm.
Includes bibliographical references and index.
1. Knowledge workers. 2. Intellectual capital. 3. Knowledge management. I. Poulfelt, Flemming. II. Czerniawska, Fiona, III. Title.
HD8039.K59E35 2011
658.4'038--dc22
2011004696

ISBN 978-0-415-67801-8 (hbk)
ISBN 978-0-415-67802-5 (pbk)
ISBN 978-0-203-80669-2 (ebk)

Typeset in Bembo
by GCS, Leighton Buzzard, Bedfordshire

Printed and bound in Great Britain by
TJ International Ltd, Padstow, Cornwall

CONTENTS

List of illustrations vii
Preface ix
Introduction xi

1 Value creation in knowledge-intensive firms   1

2 What do clients buy?   14

3 The inner workings of knowledge-intensive firms   34

4 Consistent strategy and the client   81

5 Employee capital   100

6 Shaping behavior: values and cultural modeling   128

7 Relations with clients rule strategy execution   148

8 Holistic management: the pyramid at play   167

9 Epilog   184

References and bibliography   *187*
Index   *191*

LIST OF ILLUSTRATIONS

Figures

1.1	Framework illustrating the management of knowledge-intensive firms	2
2.1	Client position	14
2.2	Individualized and standardized markets	24
2.3	'Our clients outperform the market 4 to 1'	29
3.1	The knowledge-intensive firm	35
3.2	Profit drivers in knowledge-intensive firms	37
3.3	Rates per day as profit driver in knowledge-intensive firms	38
3.4	Utilization as a profit driver	39
3.5	Leverage in consulting firm project teams	42
3.6	Value-creating processes in knowledge-intensive firms	44
3.7	Analysis projects in scale and scope markets	50
3.8	Market web for knowledge-intensive firms	61
4.1	Strategy in knowledge-intensive firms	81
4.2	In knowledge-intensive firms, quality and price are closely associated	89
4.3	The value of employee competence and client loyalty	92
4.4	The value chain of knowledge-intensive firms	93
4.5	IPA's turnover	97
5.1	Employees in the knowledge-intensive firm	100
5.2	Incentives for knowledge sharing	119
5.3	Netterstrøm's illustration of the connection between the demand-control model and stress	125
6.1	Value-driven knowledge-intensive firms	128
7.1	Relations between clients and professionals in knowledge-intensive firms	148
7.2	Confidence formula	150
8.1	Management of knowledge-intensive firms	167

Tables

2.1	Clients' requirements of consulting services	16
3.1	Short and long-term value creation in knowledge-intensive firms	36
3.2	Examples of leverage in large Danish firms	41
3.3	Goals, time horizons, and management challenges	53
3.4	Strategic components in knowledge-intensive firms	58
5.1	Strategies for knowledge sharing	121
5.2	Models of knowledge sharing	123
5.3	Netterstrøm's demand-control model	125
7.1	Markets for knowledge-intensive firms	153
8.1	Management tasks vary by market	180

PREFACE

Over the last decade there has been a substantial rise in the number of what we call knowledge-intensive firms – i.e. organizations whether private, public, or third sector constituted primarily of professionals: people with a high educational training. As knowledge-intensive firms grow to play an increasingly important role in local and international economies, it is vital that internal management styles and expertise keep pace.

Leading a knowledge-intensive workforce is quite unlike running a commodity-based business, where tried-and-tested methodologies and processes can be applied to motivate and get the best from people. Knowledge-based work relies on the unique strengths, experience, and client engagement styles of individuals employed in the firm. The core assets of the business, then, are the people themselves. Handle them badly, and they may defect or stall.

Successful leaders of knowledge-intensive firms must create meaning among and inspire their employees, to ensure high performance. To achieve this, leaders must understand how to target each employee's ambitions and challenges to facilitate their personal and professional development.

This book is the result of a common interest among its authors in the successful management of the knowledge-intensive firm, and an observation that, whether in the private, public, or third sector, this field has until now been subject to a 'management deficit'. Typically, this is because *professional* credentials have been assigned greater priority than appropriate *management* skills when appointing leaders in these organizations.

Our objective in writing this book is to contribute to the continued advancement of management approaches within knowledge-intensive firms, by examining what sets these organizations apart from other types or organizations and the required differences therefore in organizational and market strategy, business models, talent recruitment, and management, and client-handling approaches.

The book's title, *Managing the Knowledge-intensive Firm*, signals our belief that the challenge of managing this particular type of organization extends beyond that faced by most other companies. Although we argue that the requirements are complex and demanding, we are passionate in our belief that these challenges can be overcome – once recognition exists that a different approach and a certain dedication to the cause are needed.

The authors have brought to the table their own, complementary perspectives on the subject: one, as the manager of a private consulting firm with a strong research background; another, as a business school professor whose practice-based skills are fundamental to his work as he actively advises in the field; and a third, a world-leading commentator on professional service firms acting as a consultant, business school researcher and a manager. In combining our relative frames of reference, we have developed and refined a new framework and best-practice model for transforming the management of knowledge-intensive firms, which we support throughout this book with practical examples and observations gained through our combined experience of working in this field.

We would like to thank the many people who have contributed to this book, in particular the numerous people in the business community who have taken time out to share their management experience with us. We also owe a huge debt of thanks to colleagues with whom we have exhaustively dissected parts of the book. A grateful thank to Sue Tabbitt who challenged our wording to ensure that our views are readable to a large audience. Finally, we would like to extend our thanks to our publisher for supporting this initiative, providing a formal outlet for observations and conclusions which we hope will add new value to this developing debate.

Finally, we are immensely grateful to our families for their tolerance and unwavering support.

Nicolaj Ejler, Flemming Poulfelt, and Fiona Czerniawska
Copenhagen and Oxford, April 2011

INTRODUCTION

Today, being a successful leader requires highly specialized qualities and nowhere more so than among knowledge-intensive organizations, where success depends heavily on the approach, actions, and performance of key individuals.

Strong leaders must therefore be able to inspire and to create meaning and passion among their employees, to ensure high levels of targeted performance. To achieve this, they must understand how each employee envisages and can optimize their personal and professional development, so that they are able to facilitate this progression and provide appropriate support.

Yet this must be achieved in a way that fulfills the over-arching company strategy, which is not always easy when the professionals involved are highly qualified, independent thinkers with their own agendas, professional ambitions, and styles of working.

Large groups of professionals (defined as highly educated people) have a curious ambivalence in their expectations of working life, and therefore of their managers. On one hand, they demand independence and autonomy to work creatively and play to their strengths; on the other, they demand attentive management with support and coaching for continuous development, and expect their results to be recognized and acknowledged. If they are disappointed or the balance isn't right, there is a very real threat that they will go elsewhere to have their needs met.

If this happens, the impact on the knowledge-intensive firm can be great. Talented, experienced, specialist professionals are hard to replace. A loss of key personnel can jeopardize hard-won client relationships, cause a deterioration of service, and weaken the organization's brand.

This is much more than a HR challenge.

Addressing the management gap

For too long, management research and theory has been generic in nature, applying methodologies indiscriminately across all sectors. It has failed to identify the need for different leadership styles depending on the type of 'product' being offered and the type of employee driving the business. Rather, the discipline has appeared to assume that a firm of lawyers, an IT consultancy, a government department, or a hospital can be managed in the same way as a mass manufacturer.

Or until recently, certainly. Now, differentiated attention and initiatives are being applied to the professional services sector. Initially, private, consultancy-driven organizations were singled out as having special needs. In the latest development, however, the term 'knowledge-intensive firm' has been coined in acknowledgement that there are other specialist services organizations that share the same challenges and concerns as more traditional consultancy businesses. This category might include *internal* service organizations, for example, which have begun to look and behave more like external consultancies. It also includes any organization where the majority of employees are highly skilled – for example, hospitals, universities, pharmaceutical companies, banks, and government ministries.

Books on leadership and management are beginning to dedicate chapters to this category of organization, in acknowledgement that their challenges differ from those of product-oriented or low-skill service businesses.

In dedicating an entire book to the subject of managing knowledge-intensive firms whether private, public, or third sector we have gone a step further, such is the strength of our belief that knowledge-intensive firms comprise a segment with its own distinct challenges and requirements.

Cross-sector challenges

Although we recognize that many challenges will be different across the private, public, or third sector (comprising charities, the voluntary sector, not-for-profit and non-government organizations), we claim that there will also be great similarities. Differences may be dictated by differences in business drivers – for example, whether the main focus is achieving a profit, or 'best value'. Although the public sector is being driven increasingly to think like businesses as they balance their budgets and justify services, direct profit does not exist to the same degree as in the enterprise sector. The same is true of the third sector. Equally, we acknowledge that some conditions will vary both within as well as across sectors.

In spite of these differences, however, we maintain that there are many parallels that apply across all knowledge-intensive organizations, which offer learning opportunities to all managers of professionals despite sector. More often than not, the decisive factor is not the *sector* but the characteristics of the *people* working in knowledge-intensive firms, and the way in which clients draw on their services. And these people in knowledge-intensive firms have quite similar demands to and motivators in their working life.

One of our aims with this book is to contribute to the development of a shared language, and new, 'best practice' approaches to the management of knowledge-intensive organizations. We are convinced that, in the interests of optimal success, the management of knowledge-intensive organizations must unfold and develop in consistent ways across all sectors.

We hope this explains some of the deliberate generalizations we have arrived at.

For the purpose of this discussion, we have identified three main types of knowledge-intensive firms:

1. *The classic professional services firm* – providing services such as legal advice, financial/accounting services, architecture, engineering services, advertising and communications agencies, management consultancy, and IT services.
2. *The internal service organization* – providing services to a large company or public sector organization, such as human resource departments, communications departments, education departments, research and development departments, internal accounting departments, and so on. This type of organization finds itself increasingly called upon to demonstrate value in its services.
3. *Other knowledge-intensive organizations* found across the private, public, and third sectors, where the ratio of highly skilled specialists to support/admin personnel is high. This category includes organizations providing research and analysis, development, design, government policy departments, and development and training institutions, as well as hospitals and universities, banks and financial companies, medico industry, etc.

Knowledge-intensive firms and the economy

The potential impact on the economy of having well-managed knowledge-intensive firms is substantial.

Classic professional services firms are already acknowledged to account for the employment of an increasing number of people, and their contribution to the economy continues to grow. In 2008, legal services, management, and IT consulting, together with accounting and insurance, are together estimated to have been worth around $1.2 trillion globally, larger than the entire Mexican economy and only slightly smaller than India's (Czerniawska and Smith, 2010).

The financial impact of the services provided by such firms to client organizations is considered to be much greater than this, too. This is because most would expect to get back more than they had invested (on average six times the fees paid, according to 2010 UK statistics) (MCA, 2010).

Internal service functions, meanwhile, are also seen to make a tangible contribution, by improving an organization's efficiency, impact, and competitive edge, contributing to economic growth. The same can be said of specialist outsourced services, whose benefits to clients include transformed productivity.

Both directly and indirectly, then, knowledge-intensive firms play an important role in the global economy, with a steadily increasing significance to economic growth and absorption of labor. As a consequence, those companies' professional employees account for an increasing share of the labor market.

Winning the 'talent war'

To capitalize on the growth in demand for professional services – and to differentiate themselves as the market become increasingly crowded with players – knowledge-intensive firms need to develop their management capabilities to ensure they will be able to fire on all cylinders, both now and in the future. The 'war for talent', so dubbed by McKinsey & Company (2001), is particularly acute in the knowledge-intensive services industry. If a knowledge-intensive firm is only as good as its people, its long-term prosperity will depend on the ability to hold on to and to develop these vital assets.

Based on our own work and experience in this area, we have developed a practical framework for the enhanced management of knowledge-intensive firms. This will unfold across the pages of this book, supported by a range of case study examples taken from across the three categories of knowledge-intensive organizations defined above.

Our goal in developing and articulating this model is to provide both inspiration and practical advice grounded in consolidated experience, to help tomorrow's leaders of high-performance organizations develop a winning and sustainable management and personnel development strategy that addresses the peculiar needs of knowledge-intensive firms.

The journey

The structure of this book reflects the journey that knowledge-intensive firms will need to make to overcome current and future management challenges.

Chapter 1 introduces the framework we have developed to characterize the management of knowledge-intensive firms. Here, we discuss the three essential sets of parameters to manage a knowledge-intensive firm: the clients, the organization, and its employees – and the interplay between the three.

Chapter 2 takes a closer look at the role and needs of *clients* of knowledge-intensive firms: what they buy and what they expect from their service providers in terms of the way they are handled. Knowledge-intensive firms often place clients at the center of their company strategy. We offer best-practice solutions to how this might be done without conflicting with or undermining the needs of valued professionals.

Chapter 3 considers the inner workings of knowledge-intensive firms in more depth, exploring the need for and optimum development of strategy, business models, organizational structure, profitability models, systems, and culture. We then go on to discuss a range of common dilemmas faced by managers when translating *theory* and best intentions into continuous, everyday *execution*.

Chapter 4 deals with the relationship between the client and the knowledge-intensive firm. This is where the execution of strategy becomes critical. Strategic objectives of the service organization must be converted into consistent, coherent actions in terms of market development and client management. We argue that the firm must not deviate from its strategy, even in the event of a lack of business, as this may catastrophically harm the strategic identity of the firm.

Chapter 5 focusses on the needs of professionals – the core assets of knowledge-intensive firms. Here, we argue that business success relies on an ability to give equal priority to the firm's clients *and* its employees. While clients must have priority when a specific task is being undertaken, professionals should have priority when determining which particular projects to accept.

Chapter 6 then goes on to consider the relationship between the knowledge-intensive firm and its employees. Here, we examine value management, noting that managing professionals is about culture and values – guiding principles that must be brought to life and passed on through the actions of managers, backed up by visible systems and processes, including incentives and sanctions.

Chapter 7 looks at the final level of interplay – the relationship between professionals and clients. Given that, in knowledge-intensive industries, services are delivered by individuals or teams of individuals, this is the most important direct relationship between the firm and the client. Since managers are not able to oversee every interaction between professionals and clients, or decision made, it is vital that the culture and values originating at a management level are consistently carried through by professionals in their work with clients. This will set the standard for all service delivery.

Finally, *Chapter 8* draws together the themes explored in the previous chapters, emphasizing that, while management in knowledge-intensive firms depends on having a purposeful and consistent approach to clients, the organization's direction, and the recruitment and development of professionals, lasting success rests on the optimal interplay of these three critical elements.

1
VALUE CREATION IN KNOWLEDGE-INTENSIVE FIRMS

How knowledge-intensive firms differ

Knowledge-intensive firms are unique in their delivery, in that the service or product being provided has usually been tailored to the client's unique needs, following an intimate interaction with the professional who has been assigned to the project. It is during this highly individual exchange that the client's exact requirements will be assessed, and the professional's knowledge adapted and applied to the particular project.

This contrasts significantly with the relationship between a manufacturing company and its customers. Here, the output is a tangible product that has been produced anonymously in a factory, usually without any direct contact with the customer.

Although the general service industry has more parallels with knowledge-intensive firms in terms of the nature of the 'product' being delivered, this field is typically associated with *commodity* services. As a result, the majority of employees will require limited knowledge, skills, or experience – for example, waiting on tables in a restaurant or providing cleaning services. If staff leave, there is an inconvenience factor, but replacements will be found and customer service levels will suffer minimal interruption. (Not to say that personal motivation and service standards do not matter.)

Knowledge-intensive firms, by contrast, deliver specialist services provided by highly educated employees such as lawyers, accountants, communications advisors, management consultants, IT consultants, engineers, architects, HR specialists, researchers, trainers, doctors, and so on. Output is likely to require specialist skills, extensive experience, and qualifications, and a professional approach to work and clients. The professionals fulfilling these roles are much harder to find, command high salaries, and are difficult to hold on to without the right incentives, challenges, and job satisfaction. They can also be harder to manage.

The origins of value

In the case of a knowledge-intensive firm, the real and perceived value of what is being delivered will depend on how easy it is for the client to find comparable services (by specialist skill, quality, and experience) in the marketplace, and the impact of these services on the client's business.

To create and maintain this value requires clear vision and planning on the part of the knowledge-intensive firm and its leaders.

Typically, value creation in knowledge-intensive firms is delivered through a delicate interplay of factors relating to the client, the professional employees, and the company itself. The essential elements of value creation are illustrated in Figure 1.1.

Clients have a need and request a service.

Professionals deliver this service through their engagement with the client. (Because the output is highly dependent on the client's individual needs and the professional's interpretation of and response to those requirements, two apparently similar professionals or teams might produce different results.)

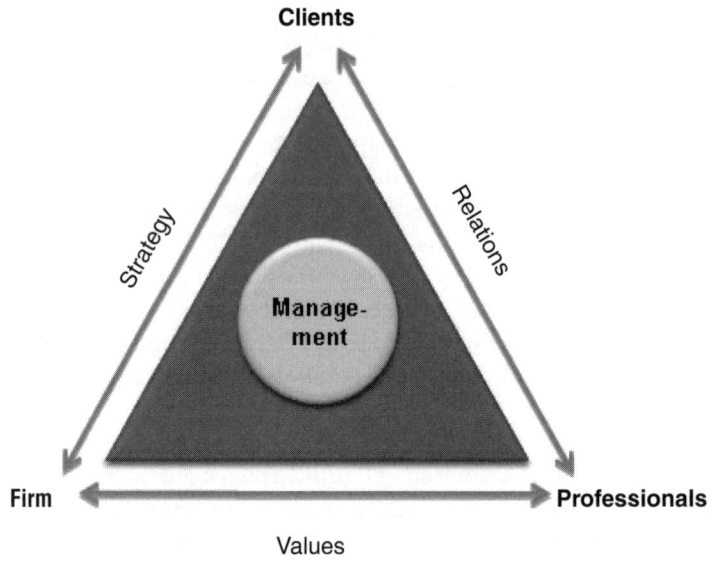

FIGURE 1.1 Framework illustrating the management of knowledge-intensive firms

The firm is responsible for choosing the work it does, targeting clients, and recruiting and managing effective professionals to deliver the services.

Successful management strategies in knowledge-intensive firms involve balancing and integrating these three cornerstones of value creation so that they ensure the strongest impact, creating optimum value. To expand on how this optimal interplay can be best achieved, our model incorporates three additional elements – strategy, client relations, and values.

The six variants, and their relative influence, are described in further detail below.

Clients

Clients have a significant influence on value creation because they define the assignment, receive the service or solution, and will be the ones to decide whether this has delivered as promised.

The solution, then, must be adapted to the client's needs and their ability to apply the solution in their organization. The level of customization involved will be determined by the knowledge-intensive firm's approach to market: standardized services based upon concepts and procedures, or customized services to be tailored to the individual client.

Matching the client's expectations will have a crucial role in determining the perceived value as experienced by the client.

The firm

The vision, strategy, and approach of the knowledge-intensive firm will have a significant bearing on the direction it takes in the market (and how rigidly it follows this), and the nature of the services provided.

Organizational factors will provide the framework for how professionals co-operate internally and with the client organization. Systems supporting service delivery (IT, knowledge-sharing, etc.); procedures for service delivery (concepts, co-operation, quality ensuring, etc.); and incentives and sanctions programs are examples of approaches and tools that can be applied to ensure quality, effectiveness, and efficiency in delivery. The company culture, driven by the firm's management, will have an important influence too.

Professionals

Individual professionals are inherent to value creation and strategy implementation, being responsible for the actual service delivery to clients. As a result, recruitment and retention of the right professionals are significant to the organization's ability to compete and position itself in the market. Crucial management considerations here can be focussed by the question: 'Who do we want to be, by virtue of the competences of our professionals?'

Professionals' demands for professional and personal development, certain types of assignments, and client relations are challenges to managers, but can be managed through career planning, skills development, allocation of assignments, evaluation of employees, knowledge sharing, and incentive schemes.

Strategy

The strategy of the knowledge-intensive firm defines the markets and the types of client it prefers to deal with. Relations between clients and the company will be dictated by the execution of this strategy by management and professionals. To ensure focus, the organization should define the type of clients it wants to go after, the services it wants to provide, and how these will be delivered (for example, by quality level or price level).

Client relations

The professionals' interaction with a client will determine the value delivered during an engagement, given that in a knowledge-intensive firm it will be the professionals themselves, and the knowledge and experience they possess, that make up the primary resource being offered. The client's experience of the engagement, based on 1) the services and products provided, and 2) the professionalism and decisions taken in sales and client meetings, and during project management, and other project activities, will affect this perception directly. Any disparity between the initial sales presentation and the actual services delivered will be noted by clients, who will ascribe more value to the actual delivery than to the expectations created at the outset.

Culture and values

The relationship between the firm and its employees is to a great extent based on the culture and values of the knowledge-intensive firm. The firm should instill these in its professionals in order to create a strong basis for their behavior and decisions in their relationships and interactions, both internally and externally. Defining and implementing this culture, and ensuring that professionals buy into the associated values, are a critical management task in knowledge-intensive firms.

Achieving balance

Effective leadership in the context of a knowledge-intensive firm involves balancing these six approaches in a way that is harmonious. The ideal is to achieve an integrated business model where all components support each other.

This book has been structured to map on to this model. In Chapters 2–7, the three primary components and their interdependencies are discussed in more detail. In Chapter 8, we step back and examine what a truly integrated approach to management requires, so that knowledge-intensive firms are assured of the best possible impact on their competitive edge, profitability, attractiveness, and reputation – both now and for the long term.

Good business starts with good people

> The people you pay are more important over time than the people who pay you (Lorsch and Tierney 2002).

Jay Lorsch has devoted years to researching the management of knowledge-intensive firms at Harvard Business School, and has published significant findings in partnership with Thomas Tierney, the former manager of global management consultancy Bain & Company and current managing director of eBay.

Through the observation cited above, Lorsch and Tierney are arguing that it is easier to find and keep clients than it is to find, develop, and keep 'star professionals' – the people responsible for securing and holding on to good clients. If you have the latter, the former will follow automatically; the same is not true in reverse. Contrary to popular belief, then, perhaps clients shouldn't always come first.

For knowledge-intensive firms, professionals are critical to success. Consequently, recruitment, development, and retention of the right individuals should be a management priority.

Attracting and retaining the best professionals rarely comes down to remuneration alone. Although every individual is different, this type of employee is likely to be driven by a genuine passion for their work, the tasks they perform, and the clients they work for. Such passion and drive are necessary to enable these highly stimulated people to function effectively over a long period of time. If the love affair falters, the firm may lose the dedication necessary to deliver the required services to deliver client satisfaction, which in turn determines and secures the firm's position in the marketplace.

Managers can create and feed this passion among their professionals by helping them to find motivation in their work. An important consideration here will be the way assignments are allocated, as professionals derive much of their passion and satisfaction from the tasks they are executing and the value they feel they are delivering for clients.

> Professionalism is predominantly an attitude, not a set of competencies (Maister 1997).

Effective leadership of a knowledge-intensive firm is to a large extent concerned with managing the individual. Since every professional is different, it is the manager's task to handle each employee in a unique and focussed way which reflects their own particular needs and situation.

Collective meetings where a manager attempts to influence culture and values are ceremonial and necessary, but not sufficient. To the professional in the knowledge-intensive firm, the more important dimension will be the individual relationship they have with the manager, and more intimate forums where there is chance to discuss individual feedback, issues and concerns, coaching, and other opportunities for further development. One-to-one sessions are important, providing managers with a valuable opportunity to inspire and influence individuals, so their priorities align with the firm's broader strategy.

Professionals should feel that their work makes sense to them: that they know where they are aiming, and why. Research demonstrates that if the firm's strategy is fully understood and bought into by professional individuals, there is a positive impact on overall performance. In other words, making sense – having a clear strategy, and ensuring that professionals understand how they contribute – is valuable to a company (Mikkelsen and Poulfelt 2009).

Motivating the individual – by distance and close proximity

The needs of the individual must not become lost in the process, however. Motivating individuals in a way that best suits their own unique needs is crucial, and just as important as having a strong over-arching company strategy. This is because effective implementation of that strategy in a knowledge-intensive firm relies on the day-to-day decisions of individual professionals in their assignments and interactions with clients. Managers can have an influence here, however, through their strategic choices about their target market and client segments. Ultimately, however, the decisive competitive parameters will be the professionals' passion for their work, their motivation to perform to the best of their ability, and the extent to which they feel supported and encouraged to do this.

Giving professionals a more rewarding work experience also means having the courage to put these intelligent, independent thinkers in a position where they have freedom to innovate and to shine. For the leader, this means being able to step back, yet without withdrawing their attention or their monitoring of requirements for ongoing coaching and feedback. Striking the right balance between management at a distance (allowing professionals to take full responsibility for their work) and close-proximity management (providing support and recognition) is a carefully honed skill, but an important one for managers to develop.

It's the execution, stupid

Combining all these requirements effectively requires thought, and then appropriate planned action. It is much more difficult to *execute* a strategy than it is to *develop* one, certainly.

Accordingly, this book is mainly concerned with execution. For professionals to execute successfully with clients, the firm and its managers need to execute effectively with their *professionals*. Our framework for successful management in a knowledge-intensive firm is designed to deliver against both these targets.

Other influences

To understand fully what makes knowledge-intensive firms tick, there are other factors to be considered, too, all of which influence what drives a company and the way it is managed. Variants include the particular market sector they are in, their ownership structures, size, profile, and clients.

Size

Are you, for example:

- a large firm with a management span beyond one manager (around 20–25 employees); or
- a smaller firm where management can be practiced in a less formalized way?

Small firms may benefit from a close-knit culture, where team spirit can thrive and the results of a shared effort are visible. Large firms, on the other hand, have the advantage of having a greater spread of competences, though differences may arise between units, and knowledge sharing can suffer.

Geographic location

Are you:

- a local firm with one or very few offices; or
- a global firm with offices in many countries?

Global firms can be attractive to large global clients – quite a different market from locally established clients. However, the global firm is challenged by delivering standardized quality to cross-cultural clients, a number of costs for international co-ordination, team configuration, etc.

Quality level

Are your services:

- of standard quality; or
- high-end (blue-chip)?

Firms with an ambition to provide a very high-quality proposition will need to ensure that their procedures and teams of employees deliver the same standard of experience every single time. If they can do this, they will have access to clients who are willing and able to pay, as well as to a strong position in the longer term. Firms whose ambitions do not reach a global level competitively should also ensure good quality, but will not face the same pressure of standardization seen at the high end.

Client adaptability

Do you strive to offer:

- standardized services; or
- customized, individually developed and targeted services?

Firms that work on a conceptual and standardized basis have an increased capability to ensure a consistent level of quality. On the other hand, they are not attractive to clients who desire very unique solutions to unique problems. This type of client is often willing to pay a premium for customized services.

Client interaction

In your dealings with clients, do you favor:

- a high degree of interaction; or
- a low level of interaction?

Some knowledge-intensive firms provide services with a low degree of interaction with the client. This may be associated with the provision of relatively standardized services, but equally this may apply to highly skilled specialist services focussed around back-office activities. Close interaction with the client will require additional social skills among client-facing professionals.

Knowledge content

Do you provide:

- a high degree of knowledge, or
- a low level of knowledge?

Advisory/consulting services can vary considerably in the degree of 'knowledge' involved. Services with a high level of knowledge are typically specialized, complex types of expertise, while lower levels of knowledge can be delivered with more standardization.

Position in the client's value chain

How critical are your services to the client's primary business:

- essential; or
- more of a support function?

Some knowledge-intensive services are aligned with essential aspects of the client organization and are therefore of elevated importance to the client. Other services are associated with more operational aspects of the client's organization, or have an impact lower down stream the value chain.

Market sector

Do you operate primarily in the:

- private sector;
- public sector; or
- third sector?

The particular blend of competences required will depend on your target client segment. Private sector clients may be looking for help with business strategy, transformational change, or workflow optimization. They may also require industry-specific expertise (e.g. in the field of telecommunications or consumer goods). Public sector clients, meanwhile, are likely to favor service providers with a deep understanding of the peculiarities of government. Third sector organizations will have their own unique requirements again.

Function

Are you providing:

- an independently provided service; or
- an internal function?

Even in the same market sector, an internal service function may have special conditions compared with an external service provider. For example, what is its competitive position (i.e. whether it is able to expand its portfolio of clients or services, or even re-form externally as a separate entity)? Other differentiating factors may include whether direct payment is required for services, whether this includes an overhead for investment and development, and so on.

Type of service rendered

Are your services, for example, primarily based around:

- analysis; or
- facilitation processes?

Knowledge-intensive services may be based around analysis or establishing a basis for client decision-making. Alternatively, they may provide more of the facilitation of processes to change the organization.

Ownership

Is the organization:

- owned by partners;
- under corporate ownership (stocks, fund ownership); or
- under public sector ownership?

Private partner-owned firms are typically very dedicated to their clients. The client is 'owned' by a partner who handles the main part of the contact with the client. This results in a systematic and deeply anchored relationship. In turn, less responsibility may be entrusted to younger professionals. Corporations are often structured more hierarchically with line management structures. Public sector organizations, by their very nature, are not about ownership. Here, management structures are predominantly hierarchical.

Challenging myths

As we begin to explore the many variables that affect the way professionals feel about and respond to their roles in knowledge-intensive firms, we begin to uncover some of the complexities that are largely unique to this field.

This will also help to dispel many of the unhelpful myths which abound about how knowledge-intensive firms should – and do – operate. In this book, drawing on the latest research and real examples, we aim to provide an alternative perspective to these assumptions. We also suggest some probing questions that managers might ask themselves to determine what may be true for their own organization, and where they might focus their attention to create improvements.

For example:

Myth:	Professionals do not want to be managed.
Alternative hypothesis:	Yes they do, if the management is good.
Question:	How do you effectively provide individual management?
Myth:	Professionals do not need to be taken care of.
Alternative hypothesis:	That may be true, but they do want to be nurtured and receive constant attention.
Question:	How can you achieve the right balance of management attention for individuals?
Myth:	Knowledge-intensive firms only have stars.

Alternative hypothesis:	No, there should also be water carriers.
Question:	How do you motivate both types in the firm?
Myth:	Knowledge-intensive firms have an up-or-out culture.
Alternative hypothesis:	No – a number of firms may *say* this is the case, but few operate this way in practice.
Question:	What are the advantages and disadvantages of an up-or-out approach? What are good models?
Myth:	Knowledge-intensive firms have a one-firm culture.
Alternative hypothesis:	On the contrary, many firms do not successfully harvest the fruits of a one-firm culture.
Question:	How can we get to that point – and what are the advantages and the disadvantages?
Myth:	Knowledge-intensive firms have strong strategies.
Alternative hypothesis:	No, most do not have a strategy that is executed consistently enough to drive the development of the firm.
Question:	What does it take to succeed with an effective strategy?

Summary

In examining where value creation begins and how it develops across a knowledge-intensive firm, we have gained our first real insight into some of the complexities involved in this vibrant and diverse industry.

Whereas the 'value' being provided by a manufacturer or general service provider can usually be seen very clearly in the standard output being provided – something that can be maintained even when staff leave or change – this is typically not true in the knowledge-intensive service industry. Rather, the quality and value of the output here are subjective, and highly dependent on the credentials, choices, and values of the knowledge-intensive firm itself and, in particular, on its professionals actually delivering the advice constituting the value creation.

It is this central difference between knowledge-intensive firms and other types of suppliers and organizations which demands a new way of thinking about leadership and management.

The pyramid model we have developed in our research, and in preparing this book, provides a useful tool to illustrate where and how value creation in knowledge-intensive firms takes place, and the extent to which this relies on the intricate interplay between the core components – the organization itself, its clients, and its people – and how this can be influenced by developing business strategy, company values, and client relations. Orchestrating the effective integration between these elements is the crux of successful management, and we believe this challenge is identical across all knowledge-intensive firms, whatever market sector they operate in.

In the following chapters, we introduce more detail as we explore each of these tenets of management in turn.

Questions for reflection

- What is your initial response to the myths highlighted here, relating to the management of knowledge-intensive firms and professionals?
- Which dimension of Figure 1.1 constitutes the main management challenge in your firm?
- Where would you rank your firm on a scale from 1 to 10 (where 1 is inferior and 10 superior) in terms of the quality of the management in your organization today?

2
WHAT DO CLIENTS BUY?

In this chapter we focus on the client as a central influence in the decisions made by knowledge-intensive firms (see Figure 2.1).

What do clients need?

It is one thing to look at what a market needs and then respond to it, but knowledge-intensive firms can and should have more control and choice than that. Indeed, their performance and profitability will depend on good decisions here.

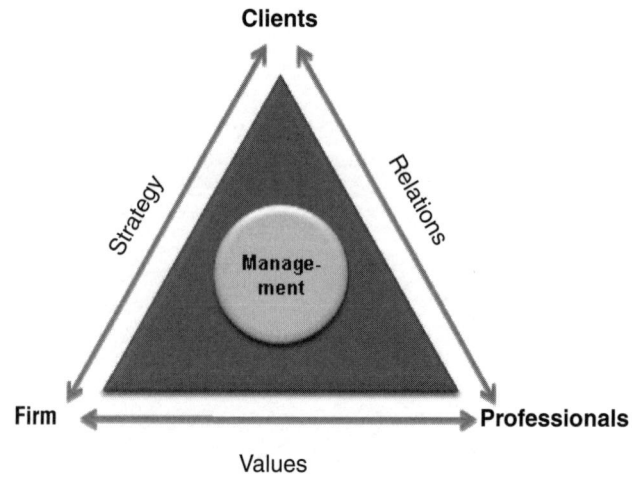

FIGURE 2.1 Client position

To lead a knowledge-intensive firm successfully, the management must define what it is good at, determine whom its target clients will be, and then optimize the delivery of the chosen service accordingly. In other words, a firm should develop a clear preference for the services it *wants* to deliver, the clients it will target, the circumstances in which it will deliver, and an optimum price bracket.

Once these fundamental, strategic decisions have been made, the firm must then design and optimize its business model to ensure that it continues to play to its key strengths and meet its own business needs, while delivering a service which addresses clients' requirements head on and meets their expectations.

Clearly, without clients there will be no business, but if that business – even with a strong client pool – is not a healthy, sustainable one internally, the risk, ultimately, is the same, so knowledge-intensive firms should choose their clients, and projects, wisely.

Clients of knowledge-intensive firms are likely to be looking for one or more of the following qualities:

- Bodies: extra capacity.
- Brains: competence.
- Brand: reputation.

When a client buys extra *capacity*, the intention is to satisfy a need for resources which the client cannot fulfill internally. The primary focus here is not necessarily buying specialist knowledge, but rather competent resources to plug a gap, perhaps because existing resources are currently overstretched. Purchasing supplementary capacity or freelance resources (often referred to as 'body shopping' in the IT world) can also be a way to avoid ceilings on the number of permanent staff. This might be a factor in the public sector, for example, or for companies owned by a global parent, or a capital fund needing to balance headcount and turnover.

When a client buys *competence*, their goal is to acquire highly specialized expertise, which only a minority of people are capable of delivering. It is likely that the client has a particularly complex problem to address for which it needs services of the highest professional quality.

When a client purchases *reputation*, they are looking for a proven, documented solution to a problem. Via the reputation of a particular supplier, the client gains access not only to experience but also to a certain security. This approach was perhaps most famously brought to life in the successful 1980s IBM advertising campaign with the strap-line 'No one ever got fired for buying IBM.'

These differing client priorities are illustrated in Table 2.1. One dimension shows the degree to which the client itself possesses the knowledge or competence necessary to solve the problem (even if they go on to procure external services to supplement these capabilities). The other dimension demonstrates the degree to which the client needs specialist knowledge or skills. This could be to anchor and develop the client's own capabilities, or to gain access to expertise which is lacking internally. Both dimensions are significant not only in identifying the client's specific need of the service but also in the way it will need to be delivered.

TABLE 2.1 Clients' requirements of consulting services

	We have the knowledge/ the competence	We do not have the knowledge/the competence
We need the knowledge/ the competence	The client should be in charge of finding the solution However, the client buys counseling because of: • lack of internal resources (extra capacity); and • a need for legitimacy via an external supplier – reputation	Competence and reputation – but involve the client to consolidate the competence
We do not need (more) knowledge/competence	Extra capacity	Competence, reputation, or extra capacity

The potential diversity of client needs highlights a number of issues which have significance for the way a knowledge-intensive firm should focus its strategy, services, price level, and competence profiles of its professionals. For example, a requirement for extra capacity does not usually elicit the same willingness to pay as, say, the need to draw on highly skilled professional expertise. This is because supplementing existing resources does not constitute the same value to the client as gaining access to highly specialized expertise. Purchasing 'reputation' will often fall in the center of the price spectrum – here, the client requires documented experience, but not necessarily highly specialized skills.

The complexity of the service will be a further determinant of the competence profiles a knowledge-intensive firm should employ and develop. This complexity will also influence the nature of the investments the organization should make in developing concepts and standardized processes, versus taking a more customized approach to solutions.

Striking this balance is a major concern for many knowledge-intensive firms. Delivering *standardized* concepts suggests a significant level of knowledge recycling, which relies on volumes of similar business, while a *customized* approach implies each client will have significantly different requirements when addressing a particular problem and situation.

The best approach for any knowledge-intensive firm will be dictated by the profile of the target client base, and preferred type of work delivered.

What do clients buy?

When clients purchase a service from a knowledge-intensive service provider – whether this is legal assistance, accountancy, tax advice, IT solutions, communications services, political advice, or administration support – gaining access to the particular service is unlikely to fulfill the need just like that. Instead, it offers *a means by which* the client's broader business needs can be met. This could be market expansion, economic gain, greater security, an improved basis for decision-making, process optimization with a view to generating more profit, greater accuracy, regulatory compliance, higher quality, or a sustainable building, to mention a few.

Given the huge spectrum of potential drivers behind each client's needs, it is possible that the client will see their challenge – and the required solution – in one light, while the knowledge-intensive firm sees it in another. For instance, a client might feel that their problem is unique, while the service provider actually has comprehensive experience in solving this type of problem, enabling it to offer a more standardized product than the client had in mind. On the other hand, the knowledge-intensive service provider might find that it supplies a unique professional competence only to find that the client draws its real value from some other aspect of the engagement.

It is important that knowledge-intensive firms understand such differences in the conception of needs and services, so that they are able to target their marketing as efficiently as possible. The client may be interested in security, confidence, promptness, legitimacy, or innovation, rather than the core service itself, for example. In this scenario, the potential success of a sale and the subsequent solution of a problem will increase once the knowledge-intensive firm demonstrates an understanding of the real requirement and suggests a clear-cut solution which directly addresses it. This is significant not only in honing the sales strategy and the concepts the firm presents to the client in concrete proposals but also throughout client relations during implementation of the solution.

'What business am I really in?' is a good question to ask to draw out the real drivers for the engagement. Project managers and project teams in knowledge-intensive firms should repeatedly ask about the client's needs and what value the engagement will produce for the client: what is the optimal result of the co-operation? To what extent might this alter as changes occur in the client's organization or surroundings?

High-performance consulting is about delivering what the client needs. Measuring success, then, cannot merely involve applying an internal professional standard to assess the degree of quality delivered. Indeed, in many of the industries in which knowledge-intensive firms operates, strong consulting and servicing of the client are not the sole expressions of the best professional standards. Ideally, the client organization should also be able to apply the product.

In some situations, it is possible to provide a good, professional service yet one which does not deliver the desired results, perhaps because the client organization is not ready or is unable to embrace the associated changes. However, this is not quality. A professional service provider should not be satisfied unless or until the designated solution has delivered the expected results for the client. The distinguishing characteristic of quality is to come up with the solution that is instrumental in addressing the client's needs and situation.

This being the case, it is the professional's responsibility to scan the client organization for political ploys, organizational barriers, economic capability, and processes or people which have an inhibitory effect. The consulting should take place on the basis of this information and focus on a solution which, all things considered, addresses the client's underlying objectives in the best possible way.

Generating client success drives the knowledge-intensive firm's business, ensuring repeat engagements and referrals. By going the extra mile to understand a client's wider issues at a deeper level, the knowledge-intensive firm will strengthen the chance of a lasting result, exceeding the client's expectations and boosting the firm's competitive differentiation. Given the continuing growth in knowledge-intensive services, this is the best strategy for maintaining and expanding market share.

Ideally, the client will also benefit from additional value throughout their engagement of a knowledge-intensive service provider. This could be simply by virtue of the co-operation process, when techniques are transferred, whether overtly or by osmosis. For example, the client may inherit a discipline of questioning requirements, to drill down into the underlying business needs; become more adept at delivering assignments on time and to budget; or better able to communicate internally.

All these factors will contribute to the overall value of the service perceived by the client. Through the client's feedback about this additional value, the knowledge-intensive firm will be able to hone further the broader service they offer as they approach and win new accounts.

Defining and refining the service proposition

Essentially, clients require three types of services from knowledge-intensive firms, defined by the degree of innovation as well as by opportunities for implementation. These are:

- innovative solutions;
- solutions based on experience; and
- conceptual and standardized solutions.

The provider will need to be clear about the main type of service it intends to deliver so that it can optimize its production model accordingly.

Development of innovative solutions

When approaching knowledge-intensive firms that present themselves as offering something innovative and different, clients will be expecting to gain access to the best and most creative professionals to help solve a unique and important problem. Only a fraction of professionals are so good that they deliver truly innovative solutions time after time. Desperate clients will call these professionals when they have an emergency. They will also be prepared to pay a premium for radically innovative solutions/services because of the additional value these offer.

American law firm, Wachtell, Lipton, Rosen & Katz, in New York, has been positioning itself as a provider of innovative solutions in its chosen field. The firm specializes in preventing hostile company takeovers, and says this on its website:

Wachtell, Lipton, Rosen & Katz provides expert service to its clients and enjoys a global reputation as one of the most prominent business law firms.

> We specialize in matters that require special attention, extensive experience, a high level of sophistication, and the reputation of our partners. We are privileged to be involved in a high percentage of the largest and most sophisticated merger and acquisition transactions, and are routinely called on to assist clients in their most sensitive and critical matters, including 'bet the company' litigation and goverment investigations and proceedings. We offer our clients an intense and highly individualized focus on their matters. (Source: www.wlrk.com, emphasis added)

A knowledge-intensive firm which sells innovative solutions can typically price its services based on their value to the client, rather than an hourly or daily rate. However, the firms who unequivocally fit into this category are few and far between.

Solutions based on experience

Other clients will be looking to purchase the *experience* of the knowledge-intensive firm, where the proposition being sold is: 'We have done this before, so the client has every reason to trust us. We have tested the methods; we have worked with the target groups; we know the business.' Such positioning provides the client with security and confidence in the given task.

Scandinavian leading engineering firm Rambøll is an organization promoting experience as its competitive edge. It employs some 10,000 people at offices internationally, including operations in the UK, India, Russia, and the Middle East, and it has worked on prestigious global projects including London Tate Modern, the North Stream Pipeline, DigiEcoCity of Chinese Gongquing, Ferrari World in Abu Dhabi, and the Copenhagen Opera and the Norman Foster Elephant House in Copenhagen Zoo. CEO Flemming Bligaard Pedersen describes the company's positioning in the following way, noting how it affects Rambøll's wider business and recruitment strategy:

> While clients do not mind paying for knowledge, they will pay even more for experience. For this reason, we have to hold on to our employees. We want to be among the largest players in every single domestic market. Our intention is to be perceived as a good old-fashioned, solid company, which makes it respectable to charge a

slightly higher fee. Obviously the client should pay for quality. This depends on the brand. The company must live up to its brand every time.

What is the driver in this scenario? The driver is that I am capable of presenting the best team to the client: a mixture of youthful passion and experience. The experience enables us to raise the hourly fees. That is the value driver of our company – convincing the client that I am weightier than the competitors. (Flemming Bligaard Pedersen, CEO, Rambøll)

Conceptual and standardized solutions

Conceptual solutions represent efficiency. This type of service is not particularly customized, so its advantage must be that it works well where it fits, the proposition being 'We have done this so many times that we have standardized and distilled the process to its purest form. This will provide you, the client, with the most affordable price for a solution that works.' Here, the client buys security in the form of a well defined solution. This is also a low-cost alternative, because it has been tested over time and is supported by procedures and IT technology to ensure efficiency.

Organizations providing this type of offering have attempted to achieve large-scale advantages through standardization. Examples from this category might include the large accounting firms that have attempted to standardize accounting methods. These companies are also characterized by high numbers of employees per partner or manager.

London and Dublin-based operational improvement consultancy, Trinity Horne, which employs around 30 people, specializes in improving productivity, particularly among front-line, client-facing staff. While experience is central to the firm's proposition, Managing Director Brendan Cahill explains that the challenge here becomes one of how to 'package' this into solutions that can be sold to multiple organizations: 'Over the years, we've worked with some of the biggest organizations in the world who value the experience we bring. But, as a small firm, we're always aware that we have limited resources and that one of our challenges is to "productize" that experience if possible.' Cahill and his colleagues therefore took some of their thinking and expertise and embedded it in a software tool (Red Owl). Julian Harper, CEO of Red Owl, takes up the story:

> Red Owl is a software application that drives productivity improvements in back-office environments. It helps organizations release operational capacity by more effective use of people and process. All back-office

functions have latent, untapped capacity: while none could realistically work at 100 percent capacity, almost all have significant opportunity to improve – particularly those where there are a large number of people engaged in transactional tasks. For years, Trinity Horne has worked with executives who struggle with resourcing plans, perhaps because it's difficult for them to forecast activity accurately, but RedOwl has codified that expertise into a management tool.

Of course it is possible that knowledge-intensive firms may cross the boundaries to encompass hybrid characteristics, particularly if there are different strands to the business.

From innovation to standardization

Naturally, the demand for product development is greatest in the market for innovative solutions, where the service must involve new thinking each time. Yet all types of knowledge-intensive firms should continuously innovate in order to remain competitive and attractive. This includes those promoting conceptual and standardized solutions, or solutions based on experience. It is crucial to develop concurrently with demand – or to create and renew the demand.

The demand for innovation is generated by a number of dynamics which necessitate innovation and simultaneously transform innovative solutions at great speed to standardized products, which again leave room for innovation.

Speed

Most markets develop at a fast pace. Knowledge-intensive firms must keep up with the market in which the clients operate, as their staff continuously develop, identify, and acquire new knowledge.

Low entry barriers

Due to the almost unrestricted access into many knowledge-intensive industries, new players will be entering the game all the time. In other sectors, this is less likely to be the case – for instance, the legal field, accountancy, and the medical sector, where special educational and professional authorization apply, if organizations are to practice legally at given levels. Even so, there is a steady stream of professionals founding their own firms, thereby creating a constant dynamism in the market.

Exchange of employees

Exchange of employees between knowledge-intensive firms contributes to the constant and expeditious dissemination of knowledge and competence in the business. An exchange of employees may also occur between knowledge-intensive firms and clients, causing knowledge and competence to be distributed in new forms. The clients thereby become qualified to take over tasks internally, that had previously been sold as a service.

Raised expectations

Clients' demands are likely to increase in accordance with their insight in how knowledge-intensive firms operate. This process also occurs via training provided to clients.

Technology

Technological development is so fast paced that knowledge-intensive firms must strive continually to sharpen and refresh their innovative edge in order to survive. Thanks to communication technology and the Internet, technology increases transparency too, as opportunities for simulations, tests, and development are made possible.

Standardized services

In terms of volume in consulting markets, relatively standardized services are dominant. Many clients require secure, proven solutions, and are willing to pay the relatively low price associated with this approach. When knowledge-intensive firms reach a size of around five professionals, the tendency to standardize often overtakes the unique customized solution. This is because there will be a need for experienced employees to work with the same type of approach, so that multiple clients can be served by the same skilled professionals. Working economically will also demand the recruitment and involvement of younger professionals, and standardized approaches are a good way of facilitating the development of younger professionals in line with company strategy.

Ongoing change

Markets, clients, and professionals rarely stand still, resulting in a constant environment of and requirement for change: 'Change and then change again' as the authors of the book, Funky Business, put it (Ridderstråle and Nordström, 2001).

Without innovation and renewal, knowledge-intensive firms will gradually or with the speed of lightning (depending on industry, market, and given situation) move from a market of high-quality services to a low-quality market in terms of knowledge and uniqueness (see Figure 2.2).

Standardized solution ⟷ **Unique solution**

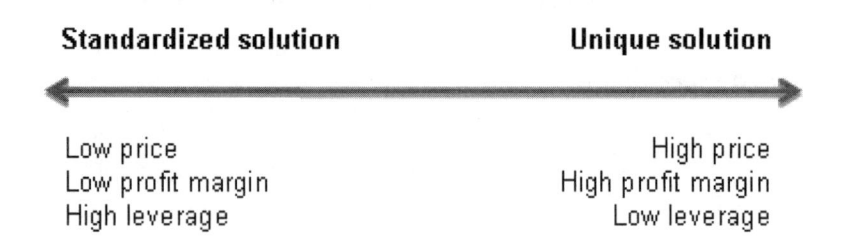

Low price
Low profit margin
High leverage

High price
High profit margin
Low leverage

FIGURE 2.2 Individualized and standardized markets

Making innovation pay

In the individualized market, the knowledge-intensive firm boasts a high degree of specialization and is likely to charge a handsome fee for its services. By contrast, in the standardized market, keen pricing is an important competitive parameter. Balancing the cost of providing the service with the premium gained from selling it is important in determining long-term success. The organizations most likely to profit are those that can transform other people's inventions and individualized services into packaged, repeatable concepts, improving their implementation.

If a knowledge-intensive firm is incapable of applying a very efficient business model, it will die. The profit margin is low, and it will be vulnerable to further impact if a client project goes awry, even to a small degree.

Some knowledge-intensive firms start out by providing unique solutions customized from task to task. However, as the firm grows and begins to capitalize on the benefits of scale, standardization tends to increase. Other firms begin by producing standardized services but, as they gain experience, move up the value chain and become capable of stepping out of the conceptual framework to participate in more individualized client engagements.

The management challenge in the individualized market is to remain on top, by continuously investing in delivering new value which can be sold in exchange for high fees. This is difficult, however, in a global age where information travels at the speed of light, and employees are seen to move readily between competitors and clients.

In the standardized market, the management challenge is to maintain efficiency. Here, firms should recruit professionals who are motivated by this trend, and nurture a culture that emphasizes reward for this kind of initiative.

In the last scenario, managers of knowledge-intensive firms must embrace the challenge of convincing ambitious professionals that standardization is okay, that it is a driver for generating profits. In the first scenario, however, the firm should ensure that unique service lines are maintained.

Service optimization

Most professionals pride themselves on delivering customized services that have been specifically tailored for each client. This sounds more valuable than a standardized offering, and suggests higher quality and greater competitive differentiation. As a result, they may perceive a career within a firm which has an individualized proposition as a better place for them to be.

Equally, many knowledge-intensive firms feel that delivering non-standardized services is the epitome of professionalism, on the basis that anyone can deliver standardization. Nevertheless, most service providers deliver standardized products to some extent. Indeed, it is our assertion that the *majority* of knowledge-intensive firms operate in markets consisting of relatively standardized services.

The trademark of most knowledge-intensive firms is their ability to deliver expertise hired by clients to perform an operation that the client cannot undertake under its own steam. Additionally, many firms brand themselves as companies operating on the basis of a certain degree of standardization – a tried-and-tested methodology they have developed, for example. This reflects a specialization and an ability to draw on experience, yet delivered at a price which most clients can afford. After all, few clients can afford or can justify paying for the most advanced solutions, nor do they have time for the intimacy and time-consuming nature of customized consulting processes. In any event, most clients find they do not really need this if they have the alternative option of a standardized approach that has been thoroughly tested and proven to be successful.

In reality, many knowledge-intensive firms tend to standardize quickly products and services that started out as tailor-made client-specific services, as their professionals gain experience in the field. This often happens naturally as professionals perform a task time after time. Best practices begin to emerge to the point where deviating from something that is known to work ceases to have any merit, other than in exceptional circumstances. By standardizing the service, the firm also becomes better able to profit from it, because it is now no longer restricted to the capacity of a single person.

At some point, most professionals realize that they are not unique experts, primarily supplying highly individual services – and that this is fine. It is possible to be a leading lawyer, consultant, architect, accountant, creative PR person, scientist, public servant, or designer without delivering unique solutions all the time. Clients accept this too. Ultimately, it is more often more comforting to them to know they are buying solid, thoroughly tested solutions.

Leveraging sector knowledge and other differentiators

Of course, standardized solutions can be supplemented with particular expertise that sets the provider apart from its competitors. This could be by combining the standardized service with relevant expertise from another part of the knowledge-intensive firm, for example, industry or sector-specific knowledge, international experience, or process expertise, which enhances the value provided to the client.

Such firms might position themselves competitively in these ways:

- Delivering high-quality solutions valued by a given industry (for example, long-term solutions, economic retrenchment, security, and illuminating analysis).
- Providing highly efficient solutions, from a rapid specification of requirements to an efficient application of resources.
- Delivering a particularly strong relationship, ensuring that the client has a good experience of the engagement, partnership and interaction. Here the focus might be on the ability to create confidence and credibility, accelerate delivery, and relieve the client in critical situations.

Although most knowledge-intensive firms operating in a standardized market tend to have relatively limited client interaction during a project, it is important that such firms develop an in-depth knowledge of their market.

There can be no substitute for this – and for applying this knowledge in an efficient business model, to enhance efficiency and optimize processes for target clients, at the same time applying the appropriate level of specialization.

Standardized knowledge-intensive service providers can generate a solid business, but achieving this depends on appropriate structuring of the business, and selecting the right clients. Managers must have a clear grasp of the premise on which the business is founded, and the profit drivers in the target industry, modeling the business accordingly. Professionals with skills and ambitions that match well with the target market should be sought out. Aim too high or too low, and there is a risk that the chosen professionals will look for greater challenges before too long, and leave.

It is not enough, then, simply to seek out the right people and hope that you can attract and employ them. The recruitment and career development strategy for any knowledge-intensive firm needs to be based on a well thought-out business strategy and comprehensive cultural modeling. Once the firm has this in clear focus, it can use the strategy to determine how it finds and develops its key professionals.

This methodical approach should include explaining and demonstrating the relevance of a given strategy and its consequences in terms of behavior of company and professionals. Which markets and clients does the firm wish to service? What sort of tasks does it want to take on? And how should these projects be solved?

'We shape a better world', is how Arup, an independent firm of designers, planners, engineers, consultants, and technical specialists, describes itself. Founded in 1946 with an initial focus on structural engineering, Arup first came to the world's attention with the structural design of the Sydney Opera House, followed by its work on the Centre Pompidou in Paris. Since then, the firm has evolved into a multidisciplinary organization. Most recently, its work for the 2008 Olympics in Beijing reaffirmed its reputation for delivering innovative and sustainable designs that reinvent the built environment.

But the challenge for any multidisciplinary firm is ensuring that the services it offers in each of its core markets are clearly articulated. Unquestionably, one of the biggest opportunities for Arup in the future will be to help its clients respond to environmental issues. Volker Buscher, one of the firm's partners, explains:

> We originally treated environmental issues as a green agenda item, focusing on compliance. But we started to feel that there was more at stake: we could help our clients do the right thing and do it more efficiently.

Saving the earth, Arup felt, didn't have to involve costing the earth, so the firm's source of added value and differentiation will come from the company's particular approach to addressing its clients' most critical issues in this area, as Buscher explains:

In our view, there are now two long-term drivers in this field. There's global warming, where clients are asking how they can make a step-change in the reduction of their greenhouse gas emissions. But there's also an organization's wider environmental footprint. Our consumption of all resources cannot keep up with growth in urban sprawl, population, and GDP. If we want to retain our way of living, these things will have to be addressed at a strategic level, not just through compliance to the latest set of regulations.

The business opportunity for Arup will differ from market to market, too:

We see a new set of dynamics in the market as firms build or refurbish property which can be sold as having a better environmental footprint than their competitors. This in turn is going to inform investment decisions: companies will be able to choose to invest in a stock of environmentally-sound property and reduce their exposure to risk. Consumers, too, will be able to exercise more informed choices.

For Arup, this all means that we are now looking at a range of services around the common theme of managing tomorrow's assets, from how you design and engineer building differently, to assessing the extent to which an organization's environmental strategies align with its business objectives. Our approach will bring together ideas for reducing costs while also dealing with climate change, an approach we've termed 'Work 2.0'.

Measuring client satisfaction

Client satisfaction is central to knowledge-intensive firms because happy clients return, recognize the value of what they are buying, and are willing to recommend the firm to other potential clients. This is particularly important given that clients of knowledge-intensive firms are typically buying intangible services whose results cannot be observed before a project begins. The buying process, then, is about trust: does the client trust that the particular provider will be able to help solve the problem? References are clearly a great aid here. Statements from existing, highly satisfied clients will go a long way in persuading a new prospect of the value they will gain by engaging a particular supplier.

David Maister, the American expert and writer on business management practices and the management of professional service firms, has documented that main drivers for high profitability in knowledge-intensive firms are satisfied professionals and satisfied clients (Maister, 2001). That the two tend to occur side by side is no coincidence. Satisfied professionals are better engaged, typically delivering the highest standard of service and delighting clients.

For this reason, focussing on developing professional's development and motivation, as well as client satisfaction, should be a priority. At the same time, and particularly in predicting future as well as current success, it will be important continuously to monitor and measure client satisfaction, employee satisfaction, and motivation as well as economic performance.

While client satisfaction can be measured through the systematic distribution of questionnaires to clients after every engagement, it will be important to dig deeper where dissatisfaction is registered. Gaining feedback here will be a valuable tool in reshaping service delivery in future engagements, or in helping the firm redefine its target projects, or the way tasks are allocated to professionals.

The American consulting firm Bain & Company monitors clients' economic performance, too – so much so that its website includes an index of its clients' share value performance measured against the market average (see Figure 2.3). For Bain & Company, the best illustration of a successful engagement is when there is a direct impact on the financial performance of its clients.

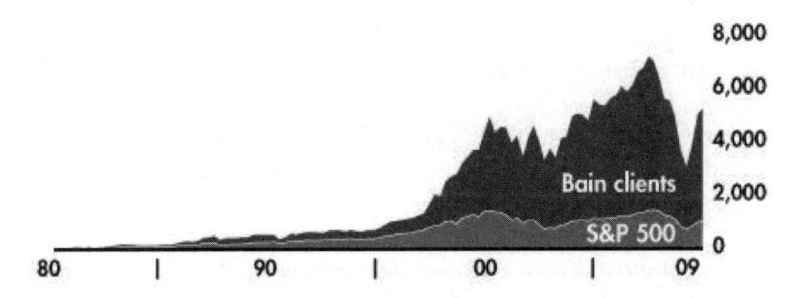

FIGURE 2.3 'Our clients outperform the market 4 to 1'
Source: www.bain.com

Measuring value created

Measuring client satisfaction is often difficult, however, because the impact of knowledge-intensive services is often intangible and its value hard to quantify. Much of the work done is likely to have an indirect, if not a direct, impact on organizations, and may be affected by market conditions outside the company's or client's control. Many knowledge-intensive services require some degree of client involvement, too, making it hard to attribute credit.

Moreover, the impact of a knowledge-intensive service may not be evident immediately, but may evolve over the months or even years ahead.

Following criticism of the use of consultants in the media, the UK Management Consultancies Association (MCA) carried out the first systematic attempt to put a figure on the value added by the UK's consulting industry. This work, which has implications for the way in which knowledge-intensive organizations assign a value to their commercial services, focussed on two key questions:

- How satisfied were clients with the work of consulting firms?
- What value had consultants added to their clients?

Satisfaction with consultants

To address the first of these questions, the MCA conducted the largest ever survey of client satisfaction with consulting services.

Consulting firms were asked to provide all the data they gather directly from clients. This was aggregated to give the MCA information on 1,800 projects. To ensure the validity of this research, firms had to send complete years' worth of data: they were not allowed to pick only those where the feedback was positive. As each firm has its own questionnaire format, common questions were identified. Response data for these questions were then collected, standardized, and weighted by industry segment for analysis.

On the whole, clients were very positive when responding to questions about the performance of the consultants who had worked for them. In 2008 (the latest complete year for which data could be assembled), 99 percent of clients said they were either satisfied or very satisfied with the work consultants did; only 1 percent said they were not satisfied. Even more encouragingly, only 2 percent of clients said they would not be willing to use the same firm again.

The news was not, however, uniformly positive. Clients' perception of value for money declined between 2007 and 2008: the percentage of people rating the consultants' work as very high value shrank from 56 to 32 percent, and those rating the work as low value increased from less than 1 to 5 percent. As there was no commensurate decline in overall satisfaction levels or any other measurement analyzed, it is likely that this perception was affected by the economic environment. In other words, clients' perceptions of value for money are not absolute: during recessions, consulting services will seem more expensive and therefore poorer value for money.

Value of consultants

The nature and scope of consulting projects vary enormously and many do not yield benefits that can be easily or objectively measured. However, it is also the value of these benefits which is particularly important when it comes to explaining the role consultants play.

To solve these issues, the MCA (2010) developed a conceptual model to describe the value consultants add. This model categorized consultants' contribution under three headings:

1. The knowledge they bring.
2. Their ability to help deliver projects.
3. The skills of individual consultants.

These facets of consulting take many different forms but, from a client point of view, they were seen to translate into three benefits for clients:

- Knowledge helps clients take better decisions.
- Experience in project delivery helps clients execute their plans more effectively and efficiently.
- The skills of individual consultants help improve the capability and teamwork of client managers.

When the MCA asked about the ways in which consultants had added value to them, clients varied in the proportion of benefits they attributed to knowledge, delivery, and skills. However:

- Knowledge never contributed less than 20 percent of the value, but never more than 40 percent.
- Delivery had the widest range, from 10 to 50 percent of the value, reflecting the fact that some consulting projects are heavily focussed on delivery, but many are purely advisory.
- The skills of the individual consultants contributed the greatest value overall, never accounting for less than 20 percent of the value and sometimes for as much as 70 percent of it.

The MCA then asked clients the following:

- How much they paid the consultants.
- Whether they judged the value the consultants added to be:

- less than they paid;
- around the same as they paid; or
- more than they paid and, if that was the case, what the value was as a multiple of the fees paid.

This approach had several advantages: it was simple to explain and retained a qualitative element, but still resulted in a measurement which could be used to calculate the overall value added. The part that worked least well was the question concerning the timeframe. This was because some projects had taken place relatively recently or, where that was not the case, many of the people involved had moved on and were therefore unwilling or unable to comment about the longer-term benefits.

Of the clients interviewed – and the MCA has been careful to point out that its research is still in its infancy – only one said that the value had been less than the amount paid to the consultants. Four said the value had equated more or less to what they paid for.

However, these proportions almost certainly did not reflect the real situation: because people do not like to discuss problems in public, those willing to be interviewed were likely to be disproportionately positive. Putting this material together with the client satisfaction meta-survey suggested the following:

- The 1 percent of clients in 2008 who said they were unsatisfied with the work their consultants undertook are likely to be the people who would judge that the consultants had cost more than the value they added.
- The 41 percent who described themselves as satisfied are those who would rate the value added as equivalent to the fees paid.
- The 58 percent who said they were very satisfied would see the value as a multiple of the fees paid.

When it came to the multiple of fee rates in this third category of clients, answers ranged from twice the fees to more than 20 times. However, the average was around 10 times the fees paid. Putting it another way, every £1 spent on consultants yielded £6 in benefits.

Summary

To be able to focus on delivering the desired services, it is vital that knowledge-intensive firms consciously identify what it is that their clients are actually asking for. Often, clients require much more than the specific service requested: for instance security, legitimacy, reliable delivery, or speed. Digging deeper, to find the contextual drivers for the particular engagement, will be important in ensuring that the service delivered is correctly aligned with the broader goals of the client. Only then can satisfaction be ensured.

The picture that is emerging in this book suggests that knowledge-intensive firms operate primarily within three categories: the provision of innovative solutions; experience-based solutions; and conceptual and standardized solutions. These propositions in turn appeal to three different markets. To optimize its organization, business model, and delivery relative to the service it provides, the knowledge-intensive firm must be very conscious of which type of services it provides, or wants to provide.

Managers of knowledge-intensive firms should embrace the challenge of a market which is inevitably and continuously pulled toward standardization, even in the case of the most innovative solutions. Market transparency, job rotation, and regular attempts at reusing knowledge and approaches all add to this pressure.

The emerging challenges, then, are these. Managers in innovative firms must accept the need continuously to innovate. Managers in experience-based firms must ensure a constantly high and updated level of experience. Managers in firms providing conceptual solutions, meanwhile, should regularly trim concepts and delivery, and find and develop new services that can be standardized.

We have argued that client satisfaction is essential to the success of knowledge-intensive firms. This being the case, client satisfaction should be measured continuously, and dissatisfied clients consulted so that the firm can learn from their complaints.

Questions for reflection

- What do your clients actually require? Why do they buy your services, and is that what your firm offers and delivers?
- What type of delivery constitutes your firm's primary focus – innovation, experience, or conceptualization/standardization?
- What do you do to protect your services from the speed of market standardization, which might undermine your business?
- Where is your firm positioned on a scale from 1 to 10 (1 being inferior and 10 superior) in terms of understanding client satisfaction, and establishing a dialogue with dissatisfied clients about the underlying causes?
- How would you value the work you do for your clients?

3
THE INNER WORKINGS OF KNOWLEDGE-INTENSIVE FIRMS

In this chapter we look more intently at the inner workings of knowledge-intensive firms. We examine *how* they generate value in the market and for clients, and how this should be built into their business model and business strategy.

In the first part of this chapter, we take a closer look at what constitutes value and how this can be created and nurtured through an optimized business model. In the second part, we emphasize the importance of articulating the vision, preferences, and goals of the organization in a strong, *executable* business strategy which is used to drive everyday decisions, from management down.

Questions for consideration as this chapter unfolds include the following:

- How, practically, is value created in knowledge-intensive firms?
- Which profit drivers should be balanced in a unique combination in the individual organization to ensure a successful business model?
- How should knowledge-intensive firms approach strategy?

Again, we draw on examples from practice to examine how firms today are pushing the value creation processes and the strategic challenges facing knowledge-intensive firms as they strive to achieve high performance.

How does this apply to me, the public sector manager might ask, yet our research confirms that these leaders too can derive value from this conceptual reflection on strategy and business models. In some public sector organizations value creation can even be compared directly with those of private companies in any case, because even here budgets and bottom line results are at play. This applies to internal knowledge-driven departments such as HR, communications, IT, and so on, which increasingly are being called upon to demonstrate their 'worth'.

In our experience, despite the potential variety of situations, a number of fundamental strategic conditions remain relatively uniform across all knowledge-intensive firms, so our recommendations should apply equally across the public, private, and third sectors when deliberating strategies for development (Figure 3.1). This is further illustrated by comments we have gathered from interviews with public sector managers.

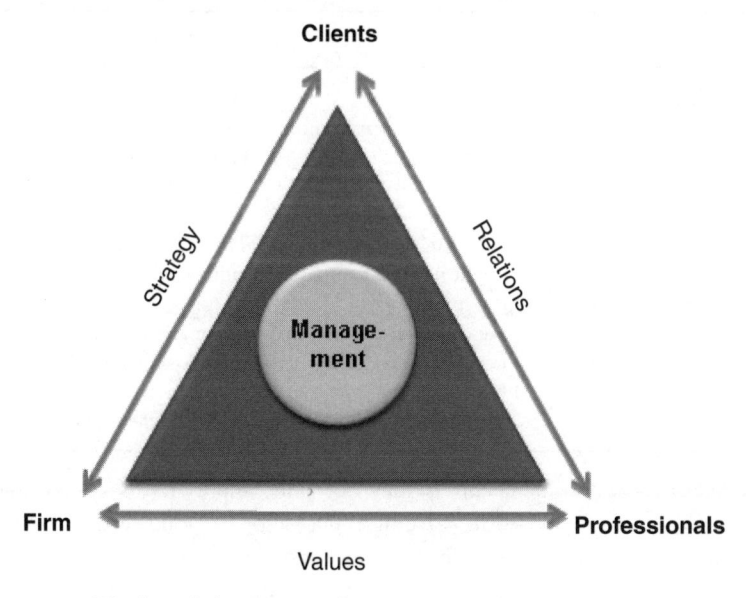

FIGURE 3.1 The knowledge-intensive firm

Short and long-term value creation

In the short term, the value experienced from an individual engagement is the profit taken away from each project, having been paid for the work the knowledge-intensive firm has undertaken. The longer-term perspective, however, assigns value to the experience gained during the engagement, which boosts the firm's skills and enhances its profile and reputation.

Any assignment will contribute to the creation of the knowledge-intensive firm's strategic identity in the marketplace (clients' perceptions of the firm's specific competence). It will also contribute to the competence development of the employees on the project team, as well as colleagues who draw on these experiences via networks and internal knowledge-sharing.

Value creation can also be negative, however. This would be the case if an assignment is not completed to the satisfaction of the client, thereby putting the firms's reputation at risk. Alternatively, the project may fall outside or on the periphery of the firm's usual area of focus, thus diverting attention from core skills and detracting from the firm's strategic identity, while consuming resources that may be needed on other (more profitable) projects. Value added by all assignments performed by the knowledge-intensive firm can be illustrated as in Table 3.1.

TABLE 3.1 Short and long-term value creation in knowledge-intensive firms

	Short term	*Long term*
Positive effect	Profits Market access/references	Development of competences Further profits Consolidation
Negative effect	Client dissatisfaction – might not want to pay the full fee Resources are bound up in tasks which could have generated income elsewhere	The reputation is influenced negatively Resources are bound up in tasks which could have generated development elsewhere

Selecting tasks and clients is thus not only important to knowledge-intensive firms' short-term earnings, but also to long-term strategic development. Managers should not only make short-term decisions about whether or not the organization has the competences and resources to take on an assignment; they must also consider whether it is wise to invest resources in the particular assignment, having weighed up the longer-term implications.

To help here, consider alternative options: which assignments could the firm potentially perform instead? Which resources need to be available if something more important/strategic/profitable comes up? These are all strategic and tactical considerations on the operational level which influence the future development of the knowledge-intensive firm. In other words, strategy is not consolidated by long-term considerations only. The current choices of operations, tasks, and focus are significant decisions which together become the *execution* of the strategy.

The challenge to managers of knowledge-intensive firms, then, is to executive their firm's strategy in the daily decisions and choices taken by not only management but also by professionals in assignments, in sales activities, in decisions on how to spend time, in human resources decisions, and so on.

Profit drivers

Business model determinants

Profitability will be created by the interaction between three central profit drivers (see Figure 3.2), which can be adjusted and combined in a unique business model to ensure financial success:

1. **Fee rate**: the level of fees that clients pay per hour or day (or according to alternative invoicing terms) is clearly a central profit driver.
2. **Utilization**: the share of hours billed to clients is furthermore of great importance to the cumulative earnings generated (since you are effectively selling hours/days) or the effective utilization of the organization's resources.
3. **Leverage**: the relationship between, on the one hand, experienced and expensive professionals and, on the other, less experienced and cheaper professionals allocated to the assignment is also of great importance to the cumulative earnings generated by the firm or the effective use of the organization's resources.

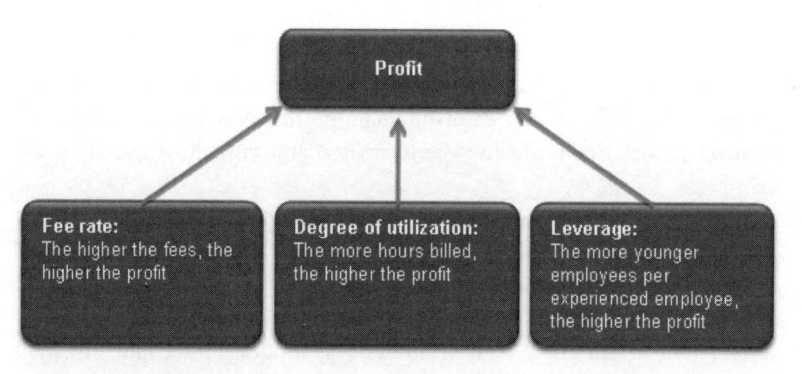

Profit

- **Fee rate:** The higher the fees, the higher the profit
- **Degree of utilization:** The more hours billed, the higher the profit
- **Leverage:** The more younger employees per experienced employee, the higher the profit

FIGURE 3.2 Profit drivers in knowledge-intensive firms

More specifically, the profit drivers encompass fees:

Fees

All things being equal, a higher fee per hour, day, week, etc., will result in higher earnings (Figure 3.3). However, the relation between rates and earnings is not necessarily linear. Rates that are too high may cause you to lose too many assignments resulting in a lack of sufficient work for the staff (utilization will be too low). However, low fees can also lead to a loss of work, since in some markets a higher price is indicative of higher quality.

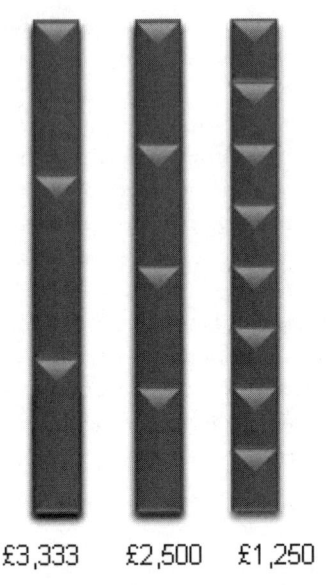

FIGURE 3.3 Rates per day as profit driver in knowledge-intensive firms

Achieving the perfect balance in a given market should result in a successful business model, ensuring high profits, whereas an imbalanced business model can cause low performance and risk the survival of the firm.

Besides billing per hour or per day, the knowledge-intensive firm may also apply value-based billing or contingency fees. Here, the price is decided by the client's value gain from the assignment. Some consultants operate with specific variants. This may mean agreeing in advance that achieving certain results will elicit a given amount of money. This could involve a basic fee which varies by or is supplemented by a certain percentage in accordance with the results of the project, or the amount may be purely results based.

International experience shows that results-based remuneration principles are used only to a limited degree. Value-based invoicing is not applied by many consultancies, but could potentially become more widespread as focus on results increases in both the private and public sectors.

Utilization

Utilization rates are calculated based on the amount of hours spent on average by professionals on client assignments, and the degree to which all these hours can be invoiced to the client (and therefore contribute to profitability). (Figure 3.4). In public and third sector firms the focus is on

Billing ratio of 50 hours week x £300 hourly fee

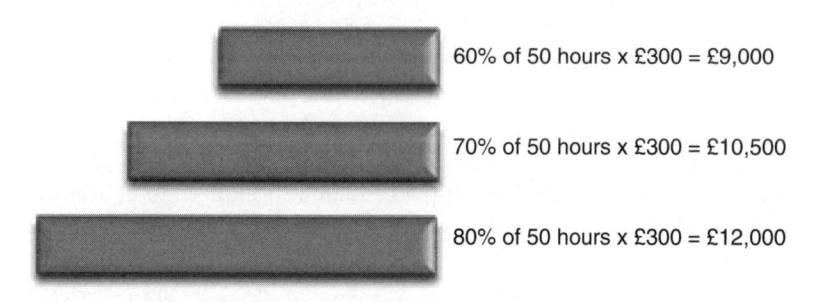

60% of 50 hours x £300 = £9,000

70% of 50 hours x £300 = £10,500

80% of 50 hours x £300 = £12,000

FIGURE 3.4 Utilization as profit driver

effective utilization of the organization's resources toward achieving its strategic goals.

In some knowledge-intensive firms, utilization is more significant to profits than fees, as utilization is about efficient application of resources. For instance, an increase in invoiced working hours of 10 or 20 percent per professional can generate more earnings than a minor increase in rates.

In knowledge-intensive firms where invoicing units are defined as hours this is not insignificant, since many professionals work much longer than the standard hours paid for. Given that many knowledge-intensive firms do not pay extra for overtime, invoicing of hours in excess of the standard week (which the professional is paid for) will contribute to the firm's profits.

Furthermore, utilization can generate earnings by optimizing the organization of production, sales, development, and of the rest of the time spent on administration, education, etc. The higher the efficiency in the execution of such processes, the more working hours the employees will be able to invoice to clients.

This is of particular importance in ensuring the efficient prioritization of sales resources, as these tend to constitute a significant share of working hours that cannot be invoiced to clients. The application of sales resources can be optimized in several ways: standardization and conceptualization; establishment of close client relations generating assignments without competition; and honed focus of sales resources relative to the type of assignments the firm chooses to pursue. Prioritizing any pitches and tenders should increase the hit rate, while freeing up hours for other, more profitable sales activities.

Too many knowledge-intensive firms expend resources on sales activities without any real potential. This may be because they are trying to sell their services in markets where they do not have sufficient competences to be a success. Alternatively, they may not be charging the right fees, or failing to meet the needs of the market − or their firm − in some other way.

In markets where knowledge-intensive firms have a hit rate of 100 percent, prioritizing which assignments to accept is also likely to be advantageous − from an economic perspective. Overstretching internal resources is a risky strategy, especially as it is expensive to train new employees, and it cannot be assumed that the right spread of skills we be available when the next client comes through the door. At the same time, firms need to be selective in the work they take on from a strategic perspective, considering how this reflects on their profile and reputation, and the extent to which − and in which areas − the new engagement will develop the skills and experience of its professionals.

Leverage

So how can knowledge-intensive firms strike the right balance?

Two of the profit drivers, fee levels and utilization, can be optimized by creating a balance between the experienced, relatively expensive employees and the less experienced, relatively inexpensive professionals. Here, the focus should be on honing this ratio, so that no senior professional is engaged in doing work which other, less expensive colleagues might do more efficiently (from a cost perspective, and in terms of freeing up the time of highly valued specialists).

Leverage ensures that all employees in the knowledge-intensive firm spend their time efficiently. This is particularly important in the case of experienced employees who often have many functions in the firm, (for example, personnel and project management, sales, client development responsibility, concept development, communications, and so on).

A focus on efficiency through leverage also creates a way for firms to take on and develop new, young employees. Some knowledge-intensive firms have a low degree of leverage (a one-to-one relation between experienced and younger professionals). Others have a high leverage with many younger professionals per experienced professional (a pyramid-shaped organization). The major consulting firms such as Accenture and Cap Gemini are characterized by high leverage; McKinsey & Company, Bain & Company and Boston Consulting Group have lower leverage, as typically do smaller, highly specialized companies.

An example of different leverage rates in Danish law firms can be seen in Table 3.2 (2010 data). The diversity illustrated in the table primary reflects that different firms within the same industry design their organizations and delivery system in various ways often related to the services offered and markets and clients served.

In recent years, consulting markets have matured and are now increasingly focusing on hiring more experienced professionals. A growing tendency is now being seen among consulting firms toward 'the rhombus' or 'the inverted pyramid' company, in place of the pyramid-shaped structure traditionally characterizing large, global consulting firms. A major driver for this is the expectation of clients to meet senior staff face to face throughout an assignment, not just at the sales meetings (Figure 3.5).

TABLE 3.2 Examples of leverage in large Danish law firms

Firm	Kromann Reumert	Gorissen Federspiel	Plesner	Lett	Bech-Bruun	Dahl
Employees	600	350	360	350	460	240
Lawyers	2320	185	200	165	230	110
Partners	59	40	47	46	62	55
Leverage	5,4	4,6	4,2	3,5	3,7	2,0

Public sector organizations, on the other hand, are using leverage to ensure efficient resource allocation in times of budget crisis and budget pressure. In some public sector organizations, leverage becomes necessary as ceilings for the maximum number of specialized staff pose a limit on hiring or appointing too many expensive experts.

FIGURE 3.5 Leverage in consulting firm project teams

Optimizing the profit driver balance

A successful business model for a knowledge-intensive firm relies on an optimal relationship between the three profit drivers outlined above. If a firm is capable of hiring younger professionals, and selling their services at the same rates as experienced professionals for example, it will be very profitable – assuming the younger professionals can be utilized at the same level as the experienced professionals.

Often, the business model of a knowledge-intensive firm will be designed in such a way that younger professionals are allocated to more client assignments than experienced professionals, while the latter also assume responsibility for sales, competence development, client service, etc. Younger professionals are also often invoiced at a lower fee rate than the more experienced professionals, who represent a higher value to the client.

Market maturity varies, of course, however. Some clients prefer a relatively higher degree of leverage to avoid paying unnecessarily high rates for solutions that could just as well be designed by less senior staff. The more standardized the solutions, too, the greater the leverage a firm can create, since younger professionals can be relatively easily trained to handle generic assignments with which they are already familiar and for which tools, approaches, and methodologies already exist.

Anders Lavesen, partner at leading Scandinavian law firm, Kromann Reumert, articulates this point well:

> We are among the most expensive [in our market], so we cannot increase our fees. Where we can increase profits will be through leverage. The billing ratio is high in our industry. In recent years, we have focussed on spending hours on development projects and

management, because we want to increase leverage. To achieve this, we need to become better managers and spend more time on internal training. We are setting up a training center to focus on learning and competence.

Clearly, managers need to find a balance, where the lesser experience of the young professional becomes profitable due to their lower salary. If the young professional spends twice as much time on an assignment as a professional who costs twice as much, there will not be much direct gain in hiring a younger professional. However, this may still be a good investment if projected growth rates are plotted against the recruitment of new employees. These factors contribute to a continued development of the organization, where the training of younger professionals is an important objective, either in terms of generating growth or to replace experienced professionals, whose indefinite loyalty to the firm cannot be guaranteed.

> Not all knowledge-intensive firms favor high leverage. American law firm Wachtell, Lipton, Rosen & Katz has deliberately opted for very low leverage, meaning a more or less even distribution of partners and 'associates' (hired lawyers who have a lower position in the hierarchy). The firm's website confirms that low leverage is a significant element in its marketing strategy to both clients (the message here being quality through close partner involvement) and potential recruits (steep learning curve via responsibility and close co-operation with partners). The wording on its home page illustrates the positive associations it has invested in this strategy:
>
>> We operate with a ratio of partners to associates far above that of our major competitors, and matters undertaken by our firm are afforded the direct personal attention of partners having expertise and sophistication with respect to the issues ... our firm has consistently ranked among the highest in the country in such categories as treatment by partners, client contact and compensation. Indeed, the level of client contact and compensation (including the base salary and year-end bonus) that we offer our associates is significantly higher than that of any other comparable firm (www.wlrk.com).

Value-creating business models

Value-creating processes

Norwegian management researcher, Bente Løwendahl (2005), illustrates how knowledge-intensive firms must establish the right business model – the right combinations of strategy and resources – to generate a successful service delivery. This must be done in such a way that a given business model balances goals, existing competences, systems, and learning and knowledge-sharing technologies. This is illustrated in Figure 3.6.

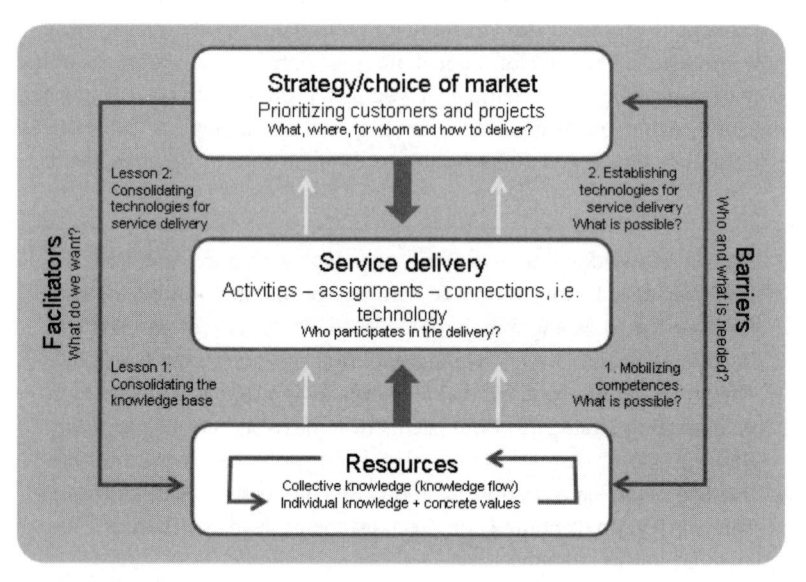

FIGURE 3.6 Value-creating processes in knowledge-intensive firms
Source: *Strategic Management of Professional Service Firms*, Third Edition, Bente Løwendahl, p. 107. Copenhagen Business School Press, 2005.

Figure 3.6 shows that knowledge-intensive firms are sophisticated systems, governed by the strategy of the firm, and the ambitions and competences of the professionals. Strategy consists of choice of market and clients (illustrated by the uppermost ring in the diagram). The strategy is supported by the needs of the professionals (the 'facilitators' on the left-hand side of the diagram). On the other hand, the strategy delimits the opportunities for development of professionals by defining market limits and the performance required by professionals in order to execute the strategy (the 'barriers' in the right-hand side of the diagram).

Strategically choosing markets you wish to work in must be operationalized into a concrete service delivery – activities, assignments, technological support (the intermediate ring in the diagram). This will be further influenced by the resources available to the firm, including professional individuals and teams (the lower ring in the illustration).

Between the rings, continuous learning processes are found. These develop the strategy and the professionals and thereby the concrete solutions produced by the firm. Of course, there will also be continual delimitations in terms of what is actually possible. Balancing strategy and professionals, then, is a central management task.

Public sector value-creation and business models

Value creation in the public sector has traditionally differed from that in the private sector, where 'profits' are clearly defined. Public sector organizations need to comply with budgets too, of course, but the bottom line is more likely to involve achieving political goals, developing policies, setting agendas, protecting citizens' legal security in case handling, and so on.

That said, public sector organizations are now becoming increasingly business orientated, attempting to apply management strategies and organizational models from the private sector to increase efficiency. Management tools such as performance contracts, results-based management, and corporate strategy are gaining popularity in the public sector as a result.

In some cases, public sector organizations are being spun off, to provide private, paid-for services in addition to the internal work they have traditionally done. The UK mapping organization, Ordnance Survey, is a good example of a public sector body whose current challenges reflect those experienced all the time in the private sector.

A knowledge-intensive public sector organization grappling with more commercial concerns is the Institute of Development Studies (IDS), a global charity for research, teaching, and communications on international development. As a charity, IDS receives no core funding from the UK government. Funding comes instead from a combination of research grants and fees from advisory work, teaching, and publication sales. The UK Department for International Development (DFID) is the institute's largest financer, but the institute also receives funds from the European Union, various UN agencies, and a wide range of aid agencies, trusts, and foundations. Many of these funds are won competitively.

Elizabeth Maddison, IDS's Director of Strategy, explains how this affects the way the organization is managed and how its services are valued:

> At the core of the institute's work we have 50 academics (Fellows) whom we employ on either a full or part-time basis. A full-time Fellow has a target of 180 days per year to be charged out on research, other contracts, and teaching our Masters and Doctoral students. Their working year is calculated at 220 days so the balance of 40 days is used to prepare proposals, keep abreast of their field, attend and present at conferences and other academic activities. Proposals are usually developed in response to funding invitations run by the UK Department for International Development, the World Bank, the Economic and Social Research Council, and other Foundations and organizations around the world. Quite a few come from governments in other countries, notably Scandinavia. These bids are all competitive on quality and price, so bids have to compete, not only against other academic institutions, but also some private sector consulting firms which do similar work and hybrid think tanks here and internationally. Like private sector consultancies, the price charged for the work covers not only the time of the researcher but the costs of running the organization – we therefore have a rate at which an individual's time is charged to a particular research contract which covers their salary, our administrative costs, and overheads and the not inconsiderable cost of securing new research contracts – winning new business and reinvesting in the institution, in effect. Unlike UK universities with research income from HEFCE, we have no core grant to set alongside a research contract to make up the total cost, but we have to remain competitive with them in many of the ways we work, the type and quality of our output, and the range, quality, and career trajectories of our staff.
>
> So in terms of the 'business model' we need to try to make a modest surplus to reinvest, at the same time as working largely for funders who are focussed very strongly on securing the outputs for their specific contract and keen to cover only the costs that they can see directly associated with that piece of work.
>
> One of the particular challenges we're facing at present, and trying to work with, is the growth in the capacity of institutions in the global south to do high-quality work in the same areas. This is a very welcome development in terms of the larger development picture, but

obviously raises interesting issues for institutions located in the global north and with relatively high costs, including salaries. Increasingly, funders are looking for partnerships between people like IDS and others in the global south and increasingly we see that as critical to the credibility of a program. We therefore have to think hard about different business models with different forms of partnership.

A further example is that of the Danish Ministry of Foreign Affairs, which has a 'competence center', UMKC, whose objective is to establish and effect competence development, leadership development, etc., among ministry staff. The center also serves other public and private companies in their competence development. As in the two UK examples, Peter Høier, Director of the competence center, describes the organization's position as akin to that of a private service provider:

> 45 percent of our turnover is generated via revenue from commercial services rendered to other ministries, companies, etc. Our foundation is the budget guide which pertains to all state-owned companies and this is a significant delimitation. Unlike private suppliers, I am unable to sell my service at the market rate, but I am obliged to sell it at a fixed hourly fee. In terms of language training, I compete with the private language schools and language businesses, semi-public or private companies, which receive subsidies and hence offer their services at a lower price than mine. For this reason I find myself in a competitive situation, where I am very conscious of the type of product I am selling. It must represent a higher value to the clients than that which they would be able to get from my competitors. I find that my competitive advantage is that I supply individual language training – or language coaching as I call it – where you are tested at entry level and receive an individual program for one-on-one sessions. In this scenario, this type of service is a bargain which the competitors cannot or will not offer – at least not at the moment.

Meanwhile, the Danish Ministry of the Environment runs its corporate administration, CFK, with a service-level agreement (SLA) approach – a widespread management tool in the public sector, comprising annual contracts based around service and price. Lotte Grünbaum, the former Head of Corporate HR at the CFK, captures the conflict of operating as a public entity with commercial influences:

You regulate via the SLA. Here you agree on which services you should deliver as a member of the service community. This would correspond to a situation where a consulting firm contracted with one company concerning all deliveries in the next year. The SLA establishes what we contribute in terms of training courses, and how many days can elapse between a course being ordered and delivered; how many days it should take to prepare a contract for new hires; how many salary payments there should be. This is very quantitative. In the years to come, a leadership development concept will be prepared.

In a consulting firm, you have the market mechanism where you can just hire more staff. Naturally, I may occasionally be able to change priorities, but I have not gathered more resources in the process. And clients do not pay. The fees are paid via an internal budget. It is extremely difficult to run an organization when you cannot apply market mechanisms. When we excel, we cannot charge more, and we cannot hire more people to respond to demand. And when clients are less than satisfied, they say that they would prefer not to pay. This is a no go. We negotiate as partners, where the SLA is the framework for the discussion. However, since everyone here is employed by the state, we cannot just fire some people and outsource the task.

Clients have felt it to be problem, that they have not been able to control the deployment of resources. We undertook an annual user survey, and of those who used our services the most were the most satisfied. However others might be of the opinion that our performance is not good enough: 'What on earth are they doing? Do they just sit around drinking coffee all day?' We in turn have the opposite experience of being extremely busy and stressed to the limit in order to optimize procedures. The reward is that our employees are asked: 'Why are your deliveries so slow?!'

Value-creating services

Knowledge-intensive firms often operate in markets with varying business models of value creation. Two such markets are that of *scale* and that of *scope*:

1. *Scale*: here, the competition and the focus of value creation concern volume (i.e. the number of identical solutions produced), since the reduction of costs per unit is a significant competitive parameter. Another competitive parameter here is experience with similar services.

As a result, lists of references with other clients are relatively significant in making sales. The competition on price may be quite intense and for this reason high degrees of standardization and utilization may be central profit drivers. Investments are primarily directed toward developing even better core services, which means a prioritization of efficiency: concepts, IT-supporting tools, etc.

2. *Scope*: this market is characterized by value creation and competition in terms of high specialization in each client, as this creates the basis for more client-specific consulting, and thereby a stronger ability to render high value to the client during the engagement. Here, the competitive parameters are a deep understanding of the client and the customized service. As a result, broad lists of references from other clients mean less than a consolidated engagement that addresses the client's individual needs. Such knowledge generates a solid confidence in the company by virtue of previous performance and knowledge of the client's situation, challenges, and needs. The competition on price levels is often less intense in this market than in the scale market, and relatively high levels of resources will be devoted to client service, which again decreases the degree of utilization compared with scale markets.

The difference between the two markets can be illustrated by the example of Scandinavian consulting firm, Rambøll Management Consulting. As Figure 3.7 illustrates, the firm operates in both the scale and the scope markets, through two different parts of the business. Both provide analysis services, supporting client decision-making.

All analytical tasks must pass through the four processes outlined in the illustration: definition of needs for information; gathering of data; analysis of data; and reporting/communicating the results to the client.

One department operates in the scale market with benchmarking analyses of organizations. These analyses are relatively standardized, and the unit's strength is in gathering and analyzing information efficiently (the two central elements in Figure 3.7). This is also true of the firm's competitors. Unique knowledge of the client is not so important here.

The other department operates within a scope market, providing policy evaluations. Here, the analyses must be designed in a co-operative effort with client and/or based specifically on the client's needs (the outer left and outer right elements in Figure 3.7). The collection and analysis of data (the central elements) are important features, but this is not where the firm's competitive differentiation lies. An in-depth appreciation of the client's needs when designing analyses and reporting the results (the two lateral elements, respectively) must be client specific and represent a high degree of applicability to the individual client, given their present challenges and options.

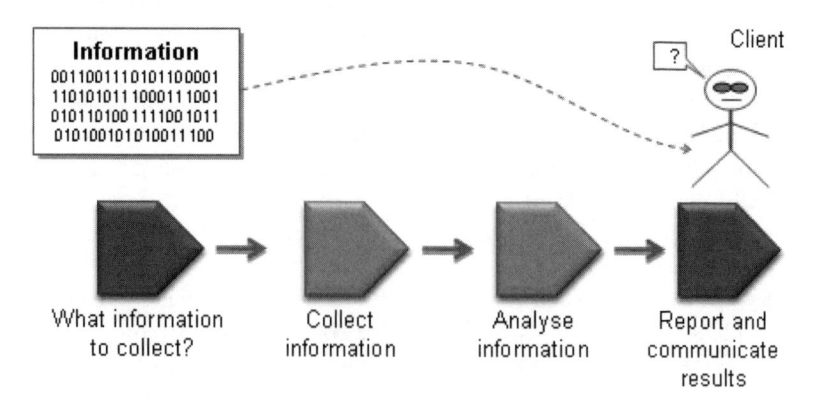

FIGURE 3.7 Analysis projects in scale and scope markets
Source: Carsten Sørensen, Rambøll Management Consulting.

Analysys Mason is a consulting firm that provides specialized research and consulting in the telecoms and media sectors, and that employs around 250 people in offices ranging from New York to New Delhi. It is an unusual consulting firm in several respects. Formed from a merger between a research/strategic consulting company (Analysys) and an engineering/operational consulting firm specializing in the telecoms sector (Mason), it retains these two sources of revenue as distinct entities. It runs research programs on strategic issues in its core sectors, aimed at helping a wide range of stakeholders, primarily in the telecoms sector, plan, invest, and market themselves. But it also offers bespoke analysis and more traditional consulting services on strategy, planning, and implementation.

Analysys Mason's research reports give the firm scale and access to a far bigger marketplace than its 250 consultants could serve in a conventional firm, while also ensuring that it remains specialized. According to Simon Jones, the firm's Vice-Chairman:

> There is a symbiotic relationship between our consulting and research divisions. Focussed on very specific sectors, the expertise we build up through our consulting work helps shape our research programs. And our research programs ensure that our consultants have a wealth of in-depth, proprietary data at their fingertips. This combination of

advice and insight is key part of our competitive advantage and has allowed us to punch above our weight with many of the biggest telecoms companies in the world. However, a key aspect of the research/consulting tracks is the need to ensure that while consulting work can shape research work, so there is a tightly defined Chinese wall between confidential client information that consultants work with and public information that research analysts work with.

The advice that knowledge-intensive firms can take from such examples is that it is important to know what market you are in and sharpen your specific competences accordingly, thereby optimizing your business model to succeed, in terms of the value you need to create for your particular firm.

In the second part of this chapter, we take a closer look at the role of strategy in ensuring the long as well as short-term success of knowledge-intensive organizations.

Strategy

We have considered the importance of the company's clarity of remit, both in terms of where and how it generates its own value, how it can hone its focus to do this more efficiently and effectively, and how this should be pulled together in an optimal, structured business model. So where does 'strategy' fit in?

Strategy represents the direction an organization chooses to ensure it remains true to its mission statement, thereby attaining its primary goals. It is where critical decisions are crystallized about what the company wants to focus on, and how this will affect daily choices – such as which business to take on, or reject.

An effective strategy requires an in-depth understanding of the market in which you operate. This means focussing on client needs; competitor competences and other driving forces significant to the competition; your firm's ability to service the market in question; and appropriate, efficient business models.

When establishing the firm's strategy, it is important to consider all the following parameters, but not in isolation:

- What do we want to deliver?
- Which markets do we want to service?
- What are our strengths?

- Which profit drivers are particularly relevant to our business?
- What are we as a firm impassioned about providing?
- What service could we be the best at rendering?
- What is our value proposition to the market (the unique service we offer)?

When assessing how the strategy should be implemented, it is important to consider the connection between the point of departure – the present position of the firm in the marketplace and its competences – and its goals. On the basis of this position, a strategy should be developed and articulated which captures what it will take for the firm to reach its goal, given its point of departure.

Goals as guiding principles

Sustainable success, defined as long-term earnings and potential growth, requires that knowledge-intensive firms have a goal and a strategy for goal attainment. An efficient strategy that is carried out and reflected in daily decisions is paramount to the success of a knowledge-intensive firm.

Knowledge-intensive firms have a wide spectrum of goals – some are primarily concerned with the realization of professional objectives; others focus on economic goals or growth. The firm's primary goal must, however, be a defining factor in its over-riding strategy, as well as in a wide range of commercial decisions, including the recruitment of professionals with a suitable profile, and a wish to participate in the realization of the firm's objectives.

Table 3.3 illustrates various goals and characteristic time horizons for implementation, as well as the challenges facing management when formulating the goals.

Like other types of companies, the knowledge-intensive firm formulates goals and designs strategies to achieve these. However, many do not achieve their goals – that is, they fail to execute their strategy.

There are two possible reasons for this:

1. The goals may be vague, their formulation imprecise, less than meaningful and motivating to the professionals. The result is that professionals do not contribute to the practical implementation of the goals in their daily decisions and behavior.
2. The fact that the knowledge-intensive firm does not have a clear goal-implementation strategy and is not ready to take necessary tactical action.

TABLE 3.3 Goals, time horizons, and management challenges

Short term	Time horizon for the implementation of goals			Managerial challenges
	Short	Medium	Long	
We should have fun (i.e. do the most exciting and developing work)	X	X	X	If short-term focus: target trends (for instance, lean, business process re-engineering, coaching) If long-term focus: long-term development perspectives
We want to make our mark in society		X	X	Combine fashionable trends with a focus on long-term development
We want to make a lot of money (profit for the owners, salaries to the employees)	X	X	X	Short and intermediate term: focus on efficiency and profitability Long term: invest in good people, dedication to strategic focus
Make a lot of money for the firm in order to create growth		X	X	Intermediate term: pursue fashionable trends, efficiency and profitability Long term: invest in good people, dedication to strategic focus
We want to be a firm with a long-term profile – an important name that survives			X	Dedication to high quality, strategic focus, investing in the best employees
We want to be the best at what we do		X	X	Dedication to high quality, strategic focus, investing in the best employees

Successful strategy is about implementing beautiful ideas. The organization must be geared up for this; it needs the right business model and the right professionals. The firm should attract people with the appropriate competences. It is also imperative that selections and de-selections integral to the strategy are implemented, since it is often tempting to make choices that do not correspond to the strategy (for example, accept business which is outside the firm's core competence and is unlikely to be a positive diversion).

Growth and development as common goals

The leaders interviewed for this book lean toward growth as the evidence and/or means by which they are both developing and achieving goals. The opposite of growth is seen to be cessation, disintegration, and lack of opportunities for realizing professional ambitions.

In many knowledge-intensive firms an important argument for growth is to ensure a consistent dynamism, as well as opportunities for professional careers. Hence the focus is often on the development of an organizational model that can consolidate these factors. In other words, recruitment, career opportunities, and the chance to reach management or partner level are central. Without this, the firm runs the risk that its key professionals will move to more tempting pastures. In this sense, growth is seen as a means by which a firm can meet these needs for personal development, by creating an opportunity to establish new management positions.

Flemming Bligaard Pedersen, CEO at leading Scandinavian engineering consulting firm, Rambøll, gives his own view on the essential connection between growth and development:

> The goal is development, development, and development. Otherwise, you cannot retain a knowledge-intensive workforce. We have to reflect the aims of our professionals. The firm cannot promote a particular profile if the professionals do not identify with it. By far the most important company resource is its workforce. For this reason, we assess our capital in terms of heads. So when we count 10,000 heads instead of 6,000, we are richer. This is where the knowledge is, and knowledge is our product. The professionals want development. If there is no professional growth opportunity in sight, you are losing value as a professional, so you find another job. That is why good employees sometimes leave us; we cannot develop them sufficiently or find management positions for them. The process is circular: with growth, we make money, but we also create opportunities for the

development of our employees. When you develop your employees, you make money. First, you create a firm that is able to retain professionals, develop them, and attract new professionals. Then you can build an enterprise that makes money.

Steve Watmough, the Chief Executive of Xantus, an independent management consultancy specializing in IT-enabled business change, takes a similar view on growth as a means of attracting and keeping high-quality staff:

> Our focus – on changing business through IT and making IT run more effectively – has put us in a strong position to grow since the firm started in 2000. We've been helped, too, by a shortage of independent experts such as ourselves. Growth is important to us, but as the means to an end not an end in itself. Success breeds success, so we find it easier to attract and recruit the best people as we get bigger. It also ensures that we have a chance to work on interesting projects for high-profile clients. Above all else, it creates a sense of dynamism and energy: we know what we want to achieve and have acquired the momentum to take us there.

PRTM doesn't consider itself to be a pure strategy firm but, rather, an operational strategy firm, with offices spanning the globe from California to China. This is how Gordon Colborn, the firm's UK Managing Partner, sees its strategy in terms of driving growth and development:

> We focus on aligning the operations of a business so that it can deliver its strategy. Our heritage is in operations management, primarily supply chain management and new product development, but some time ago we realized there was often a misalignment between the business strategy and its operations. We saw an opportunity to help bridge the gap between where they are and where they want to be by constructing and delivering an operational strategy.

This has been a winning formula: although 2009 was a difficult year for many consulting firms, PRTM grew rapidly, almost doubling in size in some parts of the world. Colborn details why:

> We'd attribute some of that success to the extent to which we can demonstrate we have added value to our clients – our research suggests that, since starting in the mid-1970s, we've added some $300 billion of

value – but also to the clarity of our proposition which has allowed us to maintain our fee rates at a time when many firms are discounting or even doing work for free. The challenge for a firm of our size is about scale: there will always be very large transformation projects where companies need a strategic advisor to help them through the process. But the role of the consulting partner is changing, from a pure advisor to someone who is willing to help clients through the process: our recent growth puts us in an even stronger position where this important market is concerned.

Public sector goals

Public sector organizations typically have a wider and more complex set of goals, reflecting the multitude of stakeholders usually involved.

The New York State Department of Education (DoE) describes itself as one of the most complete, interconnected systems of educational services in the US. This is important because of the breadth of its remit, which is to 'raise the knowledge, skill, and opportunity of all the people in New York'. Its vision meanwhile is to 'provide leadership for a system that yields the best educated people in the world'. As this implies, the DoE's role is twofold. Its operational remit is huge, ranging from the certification of teachers to overseeing education from pre-kindergarten to colleges and universities. However, the department also has a facilitating role, working with state and local governments to provide educational resources and promoting educational equity for students with disabilities, for example.

The DoE relentlessly pursues its over-arching goal of creating better results for school children. 'Failure is not an option', as Shelia Evans-Tranumn, the Associate Commissioner for the last 16 years, puts it. Schools are closed if they not perform. Principals and teachers are compensated in bonus schemes, linked to children's performance.

Another example is presented by the Office of Government Commerce (OGC), an independent office within the UK Treasury, established to help government departments and the wider public sector obtain best value from its spending. Its role, which is essentially advisory and focussed on the dissemination of best practice, has six key goals:

- Delivery of value for money from third-party spending.
- Delivery of projects to time, quality, and cost, realizing benefits.
- Getting the best from the government's £30 billion estate.

- Improving the sustainability of the government estate and operations, including reducing carbon emissions by 12.5 percent by 2010–11, through stronger performance management and guidance.
- Helping achieve delivery of further government policy goals, including innovation, equality, and support for small and medium enterprises (SMEs).
- Driving forward the improvement of central government capability in procurement, project, and program management, and estates management through the development of people skills, processes, and tools.

Buying Solutions, the national procurement partner for UK public services, is an executive agency within the OGC. Its role is to maximize the value for money derived by government departments and other public bodies through the procurement and supply of goods and services. Buying Solutions is run on commercial lines, with responsibility for generating income to cover its costs and to provide a return to the Treasury. While the OGC determines procurement policy and best practice to help the UK public sector to achieve value from its spending, Buying Solutions delivers procurement solutions for nationally sourced commodity goods and services to clients in both central civil government and the wider public sector. Yet it has no formal mandate and therefore has to earn its clients.

Rather than rely only on organizations which have provided funding in the past, part of the Institute of Development Studies' new strategy is to identify new funders and new partners in order to be able to fund work in new areas – reflecting the growing recognition that international development is increasingly influenced by non-traditional development actors outside the so-called 'development bubble'. For instance, the private sector, military, and faith-based organizations have profound impacts on development but the way they work and how this impact is realized tends to be poorly understood, and has certainly not been a significant part of the research funding mix. That raises some interesting ethical questions, says Elizabeth Maddison:

> What if a private sector organization, such as a manufacturer with a poor track record on social issues in emerging economies, was to step forward and be interested in commissioning research or want to partner with us? What if we received funding from an organization and felt the work would be highly critical of that organization? How would that sit with accepting money from such an organization? We already face situations where researchers (including sometimes our DPhil students) will come up against what might be seen as

vested interests – not just those with elected power or the power of office. Adding the financial dimension will make these issues more challenging. We have an ethics committee to help us resolve such issues, and each large proposal is scrutinized by a panel before it is submitted, including for any ethical dimensions, but discussions such as these will undoubtedly become increasingly important in the future. It is possible that individuals across the Institute may well have different and strongly held views about individual cases (Director of Strategy, Institute of Development Studies).

Strategic market and service decisions

The strategies of knowledge-intensive firms are devised and refined through a series of decisions about the services they choose to deliver to a particular market. These strategic decisions can be boiled down to the main components illustrated in Table 3.4.

TABLE 3.4 Strategic components in knowledge-intensive firms

Main strategic component	*Options for strategic choice*
Market	Customization:
	• Standardized service
	• Customized, targeted service
	Interaction with the client:
	• High degree of interaction with the client
	• Low degree of interaction with the client
	Knowledge content:
	• High degree of knowledge content
	• Low degree of knowledge content
	Position in the client's value chain:
	• High position in the value chain
	• Low position in the value chain
Type of business	Type of service:
	• Person specific
	• Concept specific
	Organization of the service:
	• Individual
	• Team

Strategic choices based on these components entail various demands to the organization, competences of professionals, incentives, pricing, marketing, and client service. A conscious understanding of the company's position on these components is central, then.

When a knowledge-intensive firm designs a business model, it should make some fundamental decisions about the type of market it wishes to serve. In addition, it should make a number of decisions about issues of a more operational nature, uniting the strategy and the business model. Such decisions could revolve around the following:

- **Nature of the service**: innovative, experience based, or conceptualized/ standardized products?
- **Type of service**: analysis or process?
- **Quality level**: top quality (blue chip) or a more 'regular' level?
- **Type of sale**: do you intend to pursue markets characterized by public tendering or a personal network-driven sale?
- **Client focus**: do you prefer to cultivate existing clients or pursue new clients from one engagement to the next?
- **Invoicing**: do you want to invoice on the basis of value, or per hour/ day?
- **Competences**: which competences would you like to develop, and what kind of professionals will you look to recruit and retain?

It is also important to consider whether there is a difference between what you believe you are selling as a knowledge-intensive firm and what clients actually buy, as discussed in Chapter 2.

Knowledge-intensive firms must decide, strategically, which markets they have chosen to service. A market can be defined via a number of elements. For knowledge-intensive firms, we have identified four basic strategic elements (see Table 3.4) which may inspire other knowledge-intensive firms in their strategic work.

Customization

Knowledge-intensive firms must determine the degree of customization or standardization of the product or the service they deliver. They may focus on a high degree of standardization, or on a low degree of standardization and thereby also a customized, targeted approach to the majority of the assignments performed.

Client interaction

Equally, knowledge-intensive firms must agree on the degree of client interaction they want to apply in their services. They may prefer a high degree of intimacy and interaction with the client, or a low-touch relationship, as seen in the provision of back-office services. Here, the firm primarily works independently when creating solutions. Only to a lesser extent does the firm exchange information with the client during the engagement.

Knowledge content

Knowledge-intensive firms must decide on the level of knowledge content provided in the services they deliver. They may go for a high degree of knowledge content, consequently investing in specialist competences. Alternatively, they may opt for a relatively low level of knowledge content, employing a more varied workforce and developing leverage and conceptualization accordingly.

Value chain

Another critical decision will be which operative level in the client's value chain to work for. A high-level focus will point to quite central services of strategic significance to the client, while a lower-level approach suggests operationally orientated services.

Creating a market 'web'

By combining each of these four key strands of a strategy, we are able to define the target market that the knowledge-intensive firm will operate in. Entwined, these critical strands will form their market 'web', where they will 'catch' their target business (Figure 3.8).

This market web can be applied to understand a knowledge-intensive firm's target market, by mapping the four dimensions and drawing a diagram where the extent of the area covered indicates the position of the firm in the market. This can be done for the firm as a whole and for specific parts of the firm, since different service areas may have varying positions, and thereby cover a number of areas. Any knowledge-intensive firm, whether in the public or the private sector, can apply this notion of a 'web' in order to understand their position and the direction in which they want to move.

While there is not a direct parallel between the extent of the area covered and quality or price level, this will often be the case. For example, on the

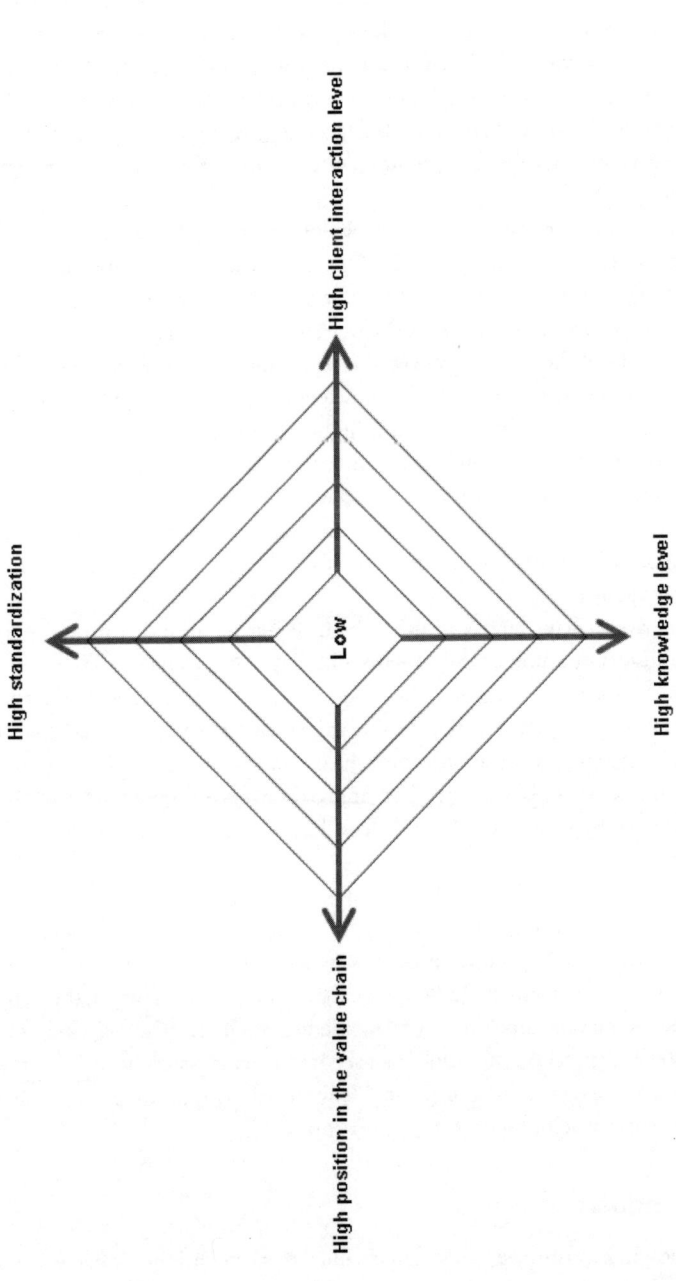

FIGURE 3.8 Market web for knowledge-intensive firms

interaction parameter: a knowledge-intensive firm may well operate with a low degree of client interaction when providing a highly specialized and very expensive service which has a strategic significance for the client. This could be the production of a highly specialized economic model, or tax consulting. On the other hand, a high degree of interaction may signify that the service is strategically important to the client – for example, strategy consulting.

In similar ways, services with a relatively low degree of knowledge content can be transformed into highly paid services – such as an off-the-moment interior designer with a highly creative flair but who has no specific training or, in terms of low-fee services, perhaps a law firm's offering to real-estate purchasers, where the service delivered is a low-priced, standard package of document handling. A high level of knowledge content, meanwhile, can be sold more or less strategically and at a higher or lower price.

Knowledge-intensive firms that claim they do not want to position themselves in any given position in the four parameters making up our web will nevertheless find themselves positioned at a certain position despite their resistance, through the assignments they accept, manage, and profile themselves against.

Indeed, many firms have a profile which relates to the main thrust of its services and business units, while a particular department may be known for the particular market it targets. Others will be known for different things to different client groups, according to the particular strand of the business. It is important not to lose focus, however. Firms and their professionals should focus on the markets where they can apply their core competences to the full – and thereby charge the highest fees. This will also ensure professional satisfaction.

Over and above the market itself, other elements contribute to distinguishing knowledge-intensive firms from each other. Knowledge-intensive firms which occupy more or less the same sector of the market may still differ considerably. Differences may emerge in terms of the type of business or market movement of knowledge-intensive firms via strategic identity (client perception). One factor of particular significance is the firm's ability to execute its strategy via daily decisions in sales, performance of assignments, development, HR, and so on.

Market models

In the following section we focus on individual markets and the characteristics of knowledge-intensive firms operating in these markets.

Customization

A *low degree of customization* is found in a market where the knowledge-intensive firm supplies standardized services based on concepts, methods, and approaches that have been developed to suit a relatively broad range of client groups. As a result, the service is not tailored to the specific client.

However, some services might be specialized in that they involve a high degree of knowledge content. Here, the service has not been designed for a particular client but as a response to a specific challenge shared by many clients in need of consulting. In large markets, a relatively limited service may still have a large client base.

Standard services often come – or are expected to be made available – at a low price. To be competitive in the market, the knowledge-intensive firm should strive to standardize and optimize all its production processes and the sale of the service. There should also be a low degree of 'waste' – that is, errors that demand extra work to rectify – to ensure that the profitability of services is not undermined. Ideally, services should be delivered in terms of known processes, which can be controlled by the knowledge-intensive firm in order to avoid surprises that might significantly raise production costs. Even small fluctuations in the predicted consumption of hours will jeopardize the business and render the assignment no longer financially viable.

We've already mentioned the standard legal package offered to real-estate purchasers. To most lawyers, this is a clear-cut, standard service, which is only viable thanks to a very efficient procedure with high leverage – i.e. there is a maximum involvement by legal secretaries or junior clerks, and minimal input from higher-paid experts.

A similar model, this time in management consulting, can be seen in global firm Accenture's outsourcing services. Accenture is very accomplished at developing efficient approaches to the delivery of its services. A particular strength is in taking new ideas and streamlining these to create standardized concept services, with optimized delivery. This enables Accenture to sell services with a high degree of standardization and leverage. This approach is relatively common in the outsourcing market, a complex field managed with standardized tools and approaches. It is typically marketed to clients on the basis that the solutions are 'proven', using known 'best practices', while also delivered efficiently and at relatively low cost.

The management challenge in markets with a low degree of customization is not to take on assignments that are too complex or too risky in terms of the firm's ability to make profits. At the same time, the firm will need to recruit practitioners who are prepared to do standardized work, ensuring that their ambitions match the tasks. Likewise, concept development, standardization, and service processes must be a key focus for investment.

At the other end of the scale are *highly customized solutions*, where the knowledge-intensive firm delivers services designed specifically for an individual client, in response to a particular combination of needs and circumstances.

Customized services are typically charged at a higher rate, enabling a greater profit margin than more standardized services. Knowledge-intensive firms make their living here by working closely with the client; as a result, the client base will usually be smaller than that for more standardized solutions. Customized knowledge-intensive firms will tend to have fewer clients, and will spend time and resources nurturing these relationships, as a successful delivery will rely on shared goals and expectations. Consequently, the service provider will need to invest in client service, and in ensuring it has highly competent professionals who are able to optimize the client relationship. Even if it is a back-office service, these will need to be designed in co-operation with the client to ensure that the desired value is delivered.

It is possible that the service, despite being highly customized, is built from a number of standardized processes – clearly, there is little point reinventing the wheel if tried-and-tested methods can be deployed as part of the overall solution. This will save time and money, benefiting the client and the service provider equally. Typically, however, these components will need to be tailored in some way to fulfill the client's exact requirements.

> US-based law firm Wachtell, Lipton, Rosen & Katz in New York City specializes in providing highly customized solutions to complex legal situation. For example, it has developed a legal option for companies exposed to aggressive acquisitions – the so-called 'poison pill', designed to ensure independence.
>
> The firm prides itself on 1-1 leverage, so that one experienced person is deployed for each junior lawyer. The latter, in turn, are hired according to specific criteria – the top 1 percent of class at the best law schools.
>
> Wachtell, Lipton, Rosen & Katz practices value-based invoicing; the number of days spent on the task do not enter into the equation. With highly specialized expertise, the firm is capable of charging high fees. Doing so demands that the company's reputation is impeccable: it must deliver the highest possible quality every time. The firm markets itself through 'thought leadership' activities including the publication of books, professional articles, and teaching in top-league universities. (The firm's website can be found at www.wlrk.com)

In markets with a high degree of customization, management challenges include ensuring the ability continuously to innovate, so that the organization is always bringing something new to the table which justifies the higher fees and differentiates the firm's solutions from those of competitors. Accordingly, they will need to invest in extensive resources, particularly the ability to field highly qualified professionals with a strong ability to understand the inner workings and higher needs of individual clients.

Client interaction

The second market differentiation concerns the degree of interaction that exists between the knowledge provider and the client organization.

A *low degree of client interaction* tends to occur in markets where the required service is delivered in the back office – that is, without close client contact. This type of assignment typically entails heavy analytical processes. The client is not involved to any great extent, since the quality of the resulting solution relies primarily on the consultancy's expertise in the field. The client, then, is not called upon to spend time consulting with the project team and in turn the professionals have less of a need to be sensitive to the particular client.

The fees paid for solutions in this market may be high or low. If the expertise is relatively standardized and could be delivered by one of a number of knowledge-intensive firms, fees will be relatively low. However, there will also be opportunities to create a high leverage – by applying younger, and relatively cheap, talented professionals. Because minimal client interaction is needed, professionals can concentrate on deploying their core skills – being valued simply because they are extremely good at what they do, knowing too that they will benefit from expert supervision in the field.

Fees are likely to be higher, if the expertise is particularly specialized, and adds substantial value that the client would be unable to replicate internally. Here, the demand on professional credentials rises too, however. More specialists will be required, and investment will need to be allocated to the development and maintenance of an expert environment.

Relatively low levels of client interaction can be seen in the outsourcing of administrative tasks associated with staff remuneration and benefits. While clearly the service will need to be designed in accordance with the client's specific conditions and options, the expertise remains with the HR outsourcing company which provides the service.

Hewitt Associates, a leader in this field, highlights this point in its marketing:

> Our integrated approach allows you to outsource your entire HR function; major components like benefits, health, and payroll; or discrete areas like absence management and flexible spending accounts, with our point solutions. Whichever combination meets your outsourcing – and business – strategy, you can be confident that you have the quality, process, and technology that come from our history of helping the world's premier organizations manage their complex HR challenges. (http://www.hewittassociates.com/Intl/NA/enUS/OurServices/ServiceLine.aspx?sln=HR+Outsourcing)

Another example of a service with low client interaction is highly specialized economic modeling, provided back office by consultancies such as the UK-based Matrix Group. It is a specialized service which only few can deliver.

Where there is a low degree of client interaction, the management challenge will be to convince clients that services have a certain value – and then to live up to client expectations. In addition to high levels of expertise in the designated field, there must be a clear match of expectations, which will involve some degree of client input at the outset.

The more scope there is for straying from the brief, and the greater the possibility that needs and circumstances could change over time, the more vital it will be to maintain close client contact, for example, with regular meetings and updates, and the formation of teams comprising people from both the client and the knowledge provider.

Assignments with a *high degree of client interaction* are typically more challenging to the knowledge-intensive firm, as this demands competent, sensitive handling of client personnel, and the ability to 'read between the lines' to ensure the brief in its fullest sense has been well understood. Even more importantly, there will need to be an understanding and acceptance that assignments with a high degree of human interaction can create greater change in the process, rendering flexibility essential (but, equally, that this 'flex' does not undermine the terms of the contract, or the provider's profit margins).

Where there is a high level of client interaction, firms will need a different approach to recruitment, too. Professionals should be capable of developing and managing multi-level relationships, and giving deeper, more intense advice. This demands skills beyond the core competences required to complete the job. As a result, the given professionals will typically be more expensive.

> American-based consultancy firm Bain & Company provides highly specialized analyses of corporate value chains, position in the market, organizational implementation, and so on. This often occurs in close co-operation with the client, in order to ensure the greatest possible application in the client's organization. This is how Bain & Co describes the scenario on its website:
>
> Bain helps companies find where to make their money, make more of it faster, and sustain its growth longer. We help make the big decisions: on strategy, organization, operations, technology, and mergers & acquisitions. Where appropriate, we work with clients to make it happen – which may mean fundamentally changing the company. Our work is most successful when we work closely with clients who are dissatisfied with the status quo. (www.bain.com/bainweb/About/what_we_do.asp)

Consultancy Xantus works in a similarly collaborative way. When Birds Eye iglo Group (BEiG) was bought from Unilever by private equity firm Permira in November 2006, it needed a new, 'fit-for-business' IT environment to support its entire sales, manufacturing, and back-office operations and workforce in the UK and across Europe – and to ensure minimization of costs wherever possible. But BEiG had a problem – it had virtually no IT staff of its own and the timing of developments was business-critical: deadlines for its separation from Unilever carried significant financial penalties. With its typically creative approach, Xantus turned the situation into an opportunity.

The situation presented clear opportunities to standardize the IT and applications, systems, and infrastructure across the group, simplify the way BEiG worked as a business, and to implement new technology and standards in a manner that would reduce operating costs. The result was a highly complex change program involving the procurement and delivery of applications and infrastructure; defining the requirements for a SAP system for the business; and the management of key suppliers. But perhaps the most complex element of the program was to manage simultaneous application and infrastructure change while maintaining continuous delivery of service – a point of failure in many similar projects.

One of the keys to success was that the chosen consulting team from Xantus combined technical expertise with a business-orientated approach.

This helped BEiG to achieve highly demanding project objectives and overcome challenges along the way. Xantus managed the entire project from start to finish; at critical points along the path its teams had the experience and aptitude to handle successfully issues ranging from procurement, through legacy systems, to system testing and implementation.

BEiG's Chief Information Officer, Tania Howarth, has this to say of Xantus's engagement:

> When you have a team of people who deliver great things and nobody is interested – or even notices – whether they are permanent employees or consultants or third-party providers, then you know you have got it right. Xantus's approach to the project was based on a genuine interest in and understanding of the issues and challenges involved, and the team would always do their best to provide an appropriate solution to any concern raised. They provided first-class program management and strategic IT and vendor management skills throughout the life of our program. As such, they have become truly trusted partners of the organization and built productive relationships with our key technology delivery partners.

In markets where there is a high degree of client interaction, the overriding management challenge is to consolidate the ability to co-create and co-operate effectively. Professionals must possess empathy and the knowledge-intensive firm should give priority time to professionals interacting with clients, both during and outside given assignments. This also means that the knowledge-intensive firm should expect to be dealing with relatively fewer clients, to ensure each receives sufficient attention.

Knowledge content

A further differentiator between knowledge-intensive firms is the nature and extent of the knowledge they provide, and its perceived value to the client.

A *high level of knowledge content* is found in markets where the service depends on specialized professionals who have been educated and trained to the top level in a highly specialized field. The high level of knowledge content can be expressed in high fees, but can also be brought into play in a market where the client is capable of performing much of the service, and where the competition is close. In such markets a high degree of knowledge will not automatically command high fees.

Services with a substantial degree of knowledge content in high-end markets demand an active recruitment profile and a competence development profile, which will ensure the maintenance of competences of professionals.

The biggest challenge to managers here is how to attract and retain this talent, given the likely ambitions of such professionals. Keeping them interested and motivated so that they do not leave the company in search of new and more exciting challenges will be a significant concern, especially if high-caliber people of the type required are hard to find.

Examples of organizations in this category are specialized legal services, involving expert competences that cannot be acquired solely at law school, and specialized engineering services, where competences are fully developed over time spent on live, complex entrepreneurial projects.

By contrast, relatively *low levels of knowledge content*, commanding lower fees, put pressure on service providers to hire generalists, thus ensuring a high leverage. They are also more likely to follow standardized delivery models, to maximize profitability.

Take the example of the Department for Work and Pensions (DWP) – the biggest public service delivery department in the UK, catering for over 20 million clients. Every working day, the DWP and the two agencies which carry out the bulk of its operational commitments (the Pension, Disability and Carers Service and Jobcentre Plus), receive around 10,000 vacancies, interview 45,000 clients to help them prepare for work, make decisions for more than 17,000 people on new benefit claims, visit around 3,000 clients, and answer over 300,000 telephone calls to its helplines. The department employs in the region of 100,000 people.

Processing benefits requires a peculiar mix of highly specialized information alongside basic administration. Increasing automation creates the opportunity to do things better, but this requires the sharing of knowledge – not just exchanging information, as Jaqui Perryer, Director of Corporate HR and HR Strategy, explains:

> We have very effective processes and systems for moving information around. We have very clear efficiency targets for processing benefits and handling queries and, not surprisingly, all our efforts in the past have been focussed on meeting and exceeding them. But the future poses a new set of challenges: can we understand the value of the specialist knowledge we've acquired as an organization and put it to better use? How can we make use of – for example – social media? Exploiting these opportunities will require a cultural change as well.

When we look at financial services companies – and part of DWP does handle vast amounts of money in the form of different benefits – we can see them setting up online communities of practice. We do have an online portal, but it's still quite a 'passive' tool. One of our challenges as we change the structure of the organization is to try and have more intelligent IT systems with information embedded in them, so that we have to rely less on the knowledge of our front-line staff and more on their generic client handling and key board skills.

This is already starting to change who we recruit: we still need to retain our knowledge but this is now more for use in the back office, dealing with exceptions and problems. For our front office, we're often recruiting people who have worked in other contact centers and who have good client service skills. Of course, these people will have a different relationship with our clients and with the rest of the department. They'll have a different set of values and will be motivated by different things – all points we will need to take into account in the future.

The value chain

A final determinant in the role of the knowledge-intensive firm is where it operates in the client value chain, and the level of impact its solutions or services are likely to have on the client's operations.

For those firms operating at a *high level in the value chain*, the service is often strategically significant to the client, requiring the need for a relationship with its top executives. Consequently, fees will often be substantial.

Firms operating in this space will typically be expected to field highly specialized competences – either technical specialization if the assignment is characterized by a low-touch client relationship, or strategic specialization in management or implementation consulting if a high degree of client interaction is involved.

> Boston Consulting Group (BCG) plays in the high-value space. The global firm specializes in supplying a strong analytical solution customized to satisfy the needs of the individual client. This is implemented in close co-operation with the client, as described on BCG's website:
>
> To us, strategy means understanding the fundamental dynamics of a business: the elements that create value and the factors that drive competitive advantage for our clients. We believe that we are

> unique in our passion for going beyond the obvious. We are not content with satisfactory solutions but rather strive continuously to generate breakthrough insights.
>
> We understand that we can build trust only if we help our clients succeed both as companies and as individuals. We strive therefore to form lifelong bonds with our clients by consistently delivering beyond our commitments and promises. We take pride in the fact that more than 90 percent of our clients retain our services year after year. (www.bcg.com)

Dublin-based Trinity Horne's work with Siemens IT Solutions and Services (SIS) provides another example of just how crucial a role a consulting firm can play. Siemens is world famous as a powerhouse in the field of electrical engineering and electronics, providing a wide range of services tailored to the needs of individual organizations. One such service is IT outsourcing, where the Siemens IT Solutions and Services (SIS) division covers everything from network and data-center services to desktop support and applications management.

Although viewing outsourcing as an important area of growth for the future, SIS is also acutely aware that global recession has been forcing huge changes on the sector. Increased competition has been making it harder for suppliers to differentiate themselves. Clients who are themselves under pressure to cut costs have been driving down margins to an unprecedented degree.

For SIS, these challenges came to a head in 2008, when it won a new account. Wresting the work from an incumbent supplier of many years' standing, SIS offered greater efficiency and lower costs. The opportunity was huge: if successful, this would be the first of many organizations looking to replace expensive outsourcing arrangements with more cost-effective alternatives. But the threat was equally huge, both in terms of financial penalties for failure and longer-term damage to its reputation. Says David Nicholson, Siemens' Global Head of Service-desk and On-ite Operations:

> When you look at a multi-year outsourcing deal, you assume that a client is locked in for the entirety of the period, but that's not usually the case. Multinational clients such as this one want global solutions, and there aren't many suppliers who are genuinely able to provide this because the barriers to entry are high. A win such as this was a once-in-a-decade opportunity for us to vault straight into the top tier of outsourcing suppliers.

Although confident in its ability to provide an efficient service, SIS was also very aware that the ultimate clients in the new account might not welcome some of the changes:

> This was a client that was moving from the equivalent of a Rolls Royce service to something that looked a bit more like a Ford. It was going to get them to where they wanted to go comfortably, efficiently, and a lot more cheaply – in fact, the cost of the contract with us was half what it had been with the existing supplier – but it wasn't going to have all the bells and whistles you'd expect from a luxury car.

To pre-empt resulting issues, Nicholson asked Trinity Horne to carry out an independent review of the infrastructure which would be used to deliver elements of the contract from a network, technology, and process point of view:

> Trinity Horne was the obvious choice. I've worked with them for 15 years and completely trust their ability to be both rigorously independent and cognizant of the sensitivities involved. Because they'd worked with us before, they didn't have to waste time familiarizing themselves with what we did and how we were organized.

There was also an opportunity here, Nicholson adds:

> We wanted to demonstrate to our client that we were finding solutions for problems even before they occurred. By bringing Trinity Horne in, we were also sending out the message that we really cared about what we were doing to the extent that we were prepared to open up our processes to independent scrutiny.

Ian Brumwell led the Trinity Horne team. Explaining the value he was expected to deliver, he says: '[The client] wanted to know what might go wrong and what could be done to head off any problems. He also wanted us to review SIS best practice and suggest areas where his team could be even more innovative.'

In their role as 'honest brokers', Brumwell and the team identified and categorized common problems, providing detailed demand forecasting to enable local managers to pre-empt problems rather than simply respond to them. As a result of the engagement, a 55 percent increase in calls was being resolved first time, while levels of client satisfaction increased three-fold, clearly demonstrating the value Trinity Horne provided through its unique independent role.

Where knowledge-intensive firms are playing up to this high level with the client's value chain, management challenges will surround gaining access to the required seniority in the client organization. The knowledge-intensive firm must develop services that consolidate this position and recruit a workforce able and willing to rise to such requirements – professionals who are dedicated to creating value for the client at the highest level. It is here, in particular, where clients will be sensitive to having a senior team pitch for the business, only to find that more junior team members are fielded to carry out the work.

A knowledge-intensive firm positioned *low in the client value chain*, by contrast, is more likely to provide services of more operational, day-to-day significance. Being less 'strategically' significant, such services will command lower fees and be more standardized in nature. Skills required will typically be more generic in nature.

One example might be a local management consulting firm, advising on the optimization of operational production processes, where the client is likely to be a middle manager. Competition is tough here, as many consulting firms are capable of delivering a similar level of service. Another example might be routine accounting assignments, which although essential to the client, are not related to the organization's strategic creation of value.

The challenge here is to recruit and develop dedicated professionals, and then to consolidate and optimize this focus in the company's solutions.

Strategic choices by industry

The market web diagram (Figure 3.8) provides an opportunity to position the knowledge-intensive firm on a relatively differentiated level of service types and markets. Furthermore, it outlines profit drivers and the importance of designing the market, the organization, and the business model in a mutually sustainable model. Only in this way will the knowledge-intensive firm be able to achieve success:

- The firm's organization and management must tally with the demands of the market.
- Recruitment and management must match the service being provided.
- Fee levels and incentive structures must match the competences required by the market.

- Pricing must mirror what the client is prepared to pay, and what is lucrative to the knowledge-intensive firm.
- Marketing and branding should reflect what your firm is, and what it offers.

The model may also inspire small knowledge-intensive firms to choose between a *growth* strategy and a *niche* strategy. A growth strategy will require a clear awareness of the chosen market to be developed, and therefore the associated recruitment requirements. A niche strategy, meanwhile, will demand conscious awareness of the chosen market segment to be targeted.

Two strategic choices must be made by knowledge-intensive firms in selecting the type of business they will go after:

1. Should the service primarily be based on people or concepts?
2. Should the service primarily be based on individuals or teams?

People or concept-based delivery

Knowledge-intensive firms can choose to base their services on either people or concepts. Among the advantages of conceptualization is the fact that the business model is optimized. Services can be made efficiently because the business model is supported by a concept demonstrating how the assignment should be approached. Furthermore, the service itself can be delivered efficiently in accordance with standards of the concept. Training of new professionals can be implemented in efficient ways because they learn a given approach. Training is furthermore supported by methods, IT systems, and procedures.

One risk of conceptualization is that the service is standardized on a level which the client does not find attractive – perhaps they prefer to be seen as a unique case, or find that the concept does not sufficiently match their current challenges and requirements. Conceptually-based services have the best compatibility in a market where clients desire proven solutions. Here, clients appreciate professionals who are able to manifest what in the eyes of the client is quality – namely, a standardized approach to solving a problem.

Above and beyond specific markets where conceptualization is attractive, conceptualization often grows when the knowledge-intensive firm increases in size and maturity. In this development, conceptualization becomes a way to ensure that all professionals deliver the service using a consistent approach.

In people-based services, on the other hand, there is a low degree of standardization of the ways in which the assignments are tackled. The knowledge-intensive firm delegates implementation to the professional, with a greater focus on the individual client and the given assignment. This may appeal to clients believing themselves to be in a unique situation. It may also be attractive in markets where competitors have availed themselves of streamlined approaches and where a particular client suddenly needs to think outside the box to set themselves apart in the market.

People-based services are typically more expensive than concept-based solutions, because a number of processes will not be as optimized. Additionally, it is necessary to invest more in development and in the optimization of personnel qualifications.

Conceptually-based services often correspond to the market web (Figure 3.8) illustration of a market based on a low degree of customization, while people-based services are more likely to correspond to that based on a high degree of client interaction. Yet, these coincidences are not consistent.

Knowledge-intensive firms with a high degree of customization are capable of working with standardized processes which are compounded to a more unique client solution. Here, the solution is designed in accordance with certain combinations of standardized competences and approaches. In similar ways, knowledge-intensive firms with a low degree of client interaction are able to work with people-based services, if the interaction involved in the assignment is closely associated with a personal relationship between the client and the professional.

Standardization is not the equivalent of a concept; it can also be a certain method or work process applied or a certain approach to the types of assignments the company takes on. Depending on the industry, standardization will be more or less in demand. Legislation, safety measures, and other regulations will entail a certain streamlining. This may occur, for instance, in the accounting sector or in the engineering industry.

The challenge to conceptually-based companies is to consolidate the support of concepts, ensuring that professionals conceptualize and apply concepts. A conceptually-based organization needs solid investments. The central management challenge facing people-based organizations, meanwhile, is ensuring sufficient quality across all assignments, as well as efficiency in every single solution.

Individual or team-based delivery

The other strategic choice that knowledge-intensive firms have to make in the consolidation of the business model is the extent to which the organization and the service delivery mode are based on individual or team efforts.

All knowledge-intensive firms have or should have a high appreciation of the individual professional. It is the initiative, engagement, and ability to develop and create quality in the solution of assignments of each professional that is the driving force in company development, the expansion of client base and market, and the career development of the professional.

Some knowledge-intensive firms focus on the individual professional to the extent that the firm's development hinges on the performance of specific people. As a result, the individual reward is considerable and a relatively individualist performance culture is created. Other knowledge-intensive firms are more focussed on team performance. Here, it is the team that is well rewarded.

There are many examples of knowledge-intensive firms that enjoy great success based on very individualized culture, management, and rewarding systems. Also, a range of knowledge-intensive firms such as law firms, consulting firms, and communication firms have a loose organizational structure – sometimes merely a shared office. These organizations market themselves under a shared company name, but in reality they prepare individual tenders for assignments and also perform the majority of assignments individually. Only if they lack sufficient capacity do they involve a colleague or a business partner.

These loosely organized firms may employ one or many people – perhaps a young professional, a student assistant, a secretary – maybe in a freelance position. In such circumstances, the individual will typically receive all the profit generated by a given assignment, with the deduction of any minor overheads to cover the community's shared expenses.

The team-based firm should not solely focus on team performance and the team-playing skills of professionals. The individual must also be rewarded, and career development with a personalized perspective should be part of the deal. However, team-based firms will stress that they need team players, because team qualities constitute a benefit to the company's overall success. The firm will not want to lose any business just because an individual employee cannot handle a certain task convincingly.

We know many managers of team-focussed knowledge-intensive firms who have even on occasion had to ask star professionals to leave the firm because they have behaved too much like lone wolves. Their colleagues were not given enough space to apply their important competences when contributing to solutions, and occasionally may have felt oppressed. In spite of high sales and client satisfaction, such stars can damage the internal cohesion of the firm, its quality, and development. Letting them go signals to all employees that autocratic actions are not accepted in the team culture.

In terms of creating long-term results, the team-based business model has typically performed well in knowledge-intensive firms. Experience shows that good professionals are attracted to knowledge-intensive firms with a strong team-based culture, and that they stay longer. It is also our belief that good professionals can gain optimal freedom in a team, provided that they are stimulated and supported when creating results. Since the professionals are the most important asset in knowledge-intensive firms, it is often wise to prioritize the team-based business model for this reason.

The one-firm firm

Many knowledge-intensive firms follow a 'one-firm firm' philosophy – that is, behaving as a single entity with homogeneous values and a culture where everyone works for the benefit of the company and each other. In American research, one-firm firms have been identified as some of the most successful, and as a result they loom large as role models (Maister, 1993). One-firm firms are characterized by a high degree of institutional loyalty, dedicated team spirit, and an uncompromising central positioning of the client. This assumes that the long-term client relationship is more important than any given assignment. Furthermore, clients and assignments are screened closely before a decision is reached about whether or not to take them on.

One-firm firms demand a great deal of their professionals. They hire only the best and spend many resources on recruitment, selection of the best graduates from selected universities and business schools, and employee development through education, training, and performance appraisals. One-firm firms primarily hire new graduates in order to develop their talents. Bonus systems are either completely universal, applying to all partners in the unit, regardless of income and performance. They may also be differentiated on the basis of varying types of partner levels (but not fully individualized in terms of each person's performance).

It is particularly interesting to observe how the one-firm approach can be established and maintained in global companies, since many offices distributed across large geographical distances and populated by employees from various cultures can present problems when trying to consolidate a single culture and set of values.

As clients become increasingly international, many knowledge-intensive firms find they must grow on a global scale to keep up with client demands and competitiveness. Central issues emerging here surround cultural understanding, international competitive competence, and legitimization among de-centralized client organizations, not just head office.

The global challenge is quite significant. In solving concrete problems in global client organizations, various cultures must be integrated in an efficient and productive approach. Furthermore, teams of professionals who do not know each other must work together efficiently and effectively. The knowledge-intensive firm culture should be characterized by mutual understanding and a willingness to co-operate. One-firm firms are often best at handling this situation. As a result, many resources in these firms are allocated to storytelling and concept development, thus ensuring unity and mutual loyalty across global units.

Many of the major global consulting firms apply considerable resources to the development of competences in order to consolidate company spirit.

> Accenture has comprehensive training centers in the US and Switzerland. However, its 'spirit' is also stimulated by given assignments, where it is the duty and responsibility of project managers to guarantee a good integration process in the team, as well as ensuring that the work modes match the company's foundational ideas.
>
> This approach is highlighted on the company's website:
>
> Accenture employees often talk about how much they enjoy working with all the highly talented and diverse individuals we have here. Variety. Learning. Teamwork. Growth. Joining Accenture translates into continual opportunities to expand on what you can do. (www.careers3.accenture.com/Careers/Denmark/WorkingHere/ & www.careers3.accenture.com/careers/global/)

Many knowledge-intensive firms would like to be one-firm firms, but only a very few actually are. It is extremely complicated to create a firm so closely knit and dedicated to implementing what it takes to be a one-firm firm. This doesn't stop them trying to emulate one-firm principles. However, processes have turned out to be very demanding in terms of management. It is not sufficient just to manifest a one-firm mindset. It must also be practiced by everyone from partner to junior consultant levels.

Being a one-firm firm is not without pitfalls, either. Professionals and management run the risk of becoming self-sufficient in their sovereignty and thereby incapable of seeing major changes in markets and client needs, which smaller and more flexible firms may be more capable of spotting. At the same time, grooming recently graduated talents may not be enough to stimulate the self-critical approach.

Nevertheless, one-firm firms have a number of strengths that knowledge-intensive firms can learn from, in particular having more than one office or even multiple locations. Value-based management and cultural mediation competences are essential.

Summary

Across this chapter, we have noted a number of important issues that knowledge-intensive firms should be aware of when sharpening their market focus.

The challenge to managers of knowledge-intensive firms is to execute their firm's strategy through the daily decisions and choices taken by not only management but also by professionals in assignments, in sales activities, and in decisions on how to spend time, and in human resources decisions.

We have noted that value creation can occur in negative as well as in positive ways, and in long as well as short-term perspectives. When assessing whether to accept or go for a new assignment, managers must consider potential profit, competence development, knowledge gain, and market positioning. This should be done against the corresponding potential risk of a bad financial outcome, of resources becoming tied up on inappropriate tasks, and the potential damage to the brand resulting from a poorly matched project. Give or take a few adjustments, these are the conditions which public as well as private sector organizations are exposed to.

As we have seen, too, knowledge-intensive firms have three fundamental profit drivers – fee rates, utilization, and leverage – the balance between which creates the founding business model in a knowledge-intensive firm. An awareness of what the market demands and where the firm should position itself in the market is, likewise, central to a firm's success.

The strategy, the business model, and the organization must work in harmony, mirroring the needs of the market in which the knowledge-intensive firm wishes to position itself. Our market web model provides a useful tool here in helping a firm to find its bearings in relation to four central dimensions:

- Customization – high/low.
- Client interaction – high/low.
- Knowledge content – high/low.
- The client's value chain – high/low.

Additionally, knowledge-intensive firms must determine whether they want to market their services primarily based on their people or the concepts they are delivering, and whether the company should primarily be structured around the individual or a team.

Questions for reflection

- Before taking on a new assignment, do you consider whether or not the task will tie up resources that could be applied in other and perhaps more strategic ways?
- Where is your firm positioned on a scale from 1 to 10 (1 being inferior and 10 superior) in terms of having an optimal business model – that is, a balance between fee rate (price per unit), utilization (optimal allocation of resources), and leverage (ratio between experienced, more expensive and younger, less expensive)?
- Try to position your firm in our market web. Is this where you want to be?

4
CONSISTENT STRATEGY AND THE CLIENT

In this chapter, our focus is the relationship between knowledge-intensive firms and their clients – exploring strategy in relation to a firm's target market (Figure 4.1) and how this should be executed on a day-to-day basis in dealings with clients to ensure that business focus is maintained.

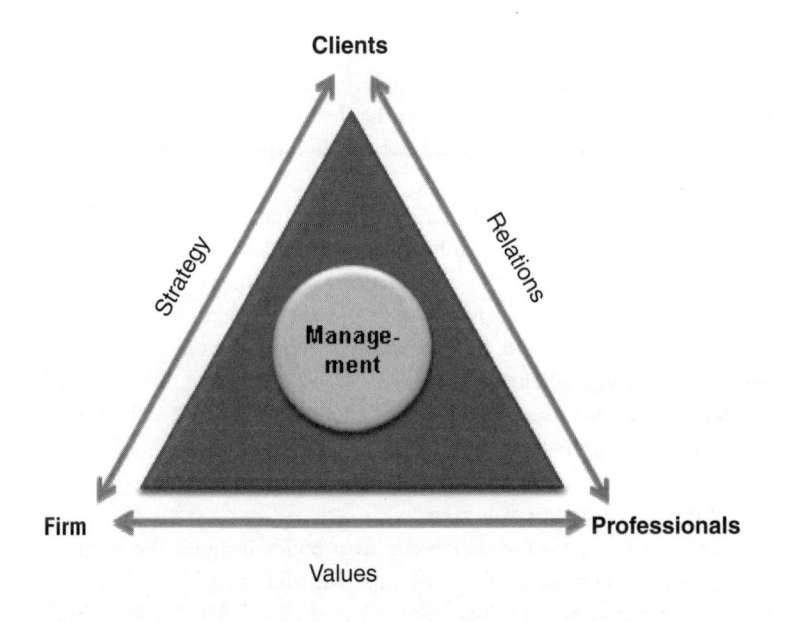

FIGURE 4.1 Strategy in knowledge-intensive firms

Deciding what you are – and what you are not

Establishing a clear strategy has far-reaching consequences for a knowledge-intensive firm. First, it will be important to establish a connection between the strategy and the organization's chosen business model. Then, a connection between strategy and practice will need to be consolidated.

Knowledge-intensive firms face two central strategic decisions when attempting to control company development, versus simply flowing with the market:

1. Arriving at a solid and cohesive strategy.
2. Maintaining a sustained focus on the execution of the strategy in day-to-day decisions – in sales, solutions, development, HR policy, etc.

Knowledge-intensive firms do not tend unilaterally to pursue one specific goal, with one type of business, in one well-defined market, and on one quality level. Rather, they will operate in a combination of these fields. However, they are likely to have a preferred focus on certain parameters, and a more clearly defined profile and particularly strong credentials in certain areas.

Making conscious, coherent choices about fundamental aspects of strategy is essential, particularly in relation to the type of market the firm wants to serve. Without a clear vision, the firm will be much more vulnerable: without a firm identity, it will struggle to develop and maintain a strong brand and reputation. It will also be harder for the firm to position itself at the higher end of the spectrum, where high quality has the potential to command premium rates.

Conscious prioritization of target markets and target business provides greater opportunities for establishing a well founded firm that has cohesion and synergy between goals, organization, recruitment, competence, and pricing structure. Clear decisions here present an opportunity to control the profile of the firm and, by extension, its strategic identity – namely, the way it is perceived by clients.

Strategic identity, then, defines how clients will see and value the firm. Essentially, a firm's strategic identity is established through:

- the types of assignment it takes on;
- the competence profile which the firm builds through the recruitment and development of professional expertise and experience; and
- the quality and performance demonstrated by the firm in the delivery of assignments.

To some knowledge-intensive firms, it may seem more attractive to flow with the market – to be led by emerging opportunities, seeing where they take the firm. However, from a long-term strategic perspective, this can be dangerous. The risk of not seeing the development of the market clearly enough and at an early stage is considerable, increasing the potential for failure. The risk of ending up in a price-sensitive market also increases because, without a clear vision and focus, it will be harder to build a profile aligned with a given area of expertise and specialization, industry, service, or approach.

A volume, price-driven market might be lucrative, if the firm has a clear conception of the business model and the types of profit drivers and effective modes of operation it should apply. Profitability will be lower, however, necessitating that the production and delivery of the service is tight – i.e. optimized and standardized – to avoid expending too much time and resource, thus eating into the available margin. Poor calculations, underestimating the scale of the job, or a need to go back and rework something can be catastrophic, undermining the firm's ability to make money. Firms playing in this market will only do well if they have planned strategically to be here and have structured their business model accordingly.

The alternative to being reactive, and flowing with the market, is to take control of where the firm looks for business, and what type of business this should be. Such decisions should then form the basis of a business model, which clearly sets out the goals and values of the firm, its processes, and its configuration of and strategy for recruiting and managing personnel.

By taking control and having a clear idea of what it will and won't do, the firm assumes greater responsibility for its fate and will be able to steer itself away from the risks facing firms with a more defensive, take-it-as-it-comes 'strategy'. As a result, every project should count, not only toward profitability, but toward building the business, brand, and market profile that the firm is striving toward.

Staying true to strategy

Of course, there is little point having a carefully laid out strategy if the business hasn't been set up to follow it. For a strategy to have any tangible impact, it must be grounded in everyday practice. Failure to live up to strategy is a common cause of poor business performance among knowledge-intensive firms.

For a strategy to be effective, it must be implemented in everyday decisions, whether these concern recruitment, remuneration, the types of assignments taken on or even pitched for, terms agreed to, and the staff allocated to the task. Additional considerations include operational decisions about the method of delivery, professionalism, client relations, and the people selected as partners if the firm has this type of ownership structure or other management positions.

Challenges and changes to strategy

It is likely that the strategy will evolve and change too, with implications for everyday decision-making. As new opportunities present themselves, the firm will need to consider the relative merits of deviating from their carefully defined strategy. Triggers may include the following:

- existing clients requesting the delivery of services not encompassed by the existing strategy;
- the potential to work with a new client, which represents a new account and potential new source of income;
- professionals finding a potential new assignment exciting, or wanting to win new business to meet a given target or keep the pipeline full;
- clients' attempts to negotiate on price;
- partners, with their own agenda, challenging or deliberately misinterpreting existing strategy parameters.

Standing firm on original strategy decisions can be difficult under many of these circumstances, forcing a rethink. A particularly challenging scenario is when a client presents a project which falls outside the given parameters of the existing strategy, but offers the possibility of leading to more lucrative, profile-fitting work later on.

Should the firm be strong, turning down the (probably unprofitable) first task, at the risk of ruling out future earning potential and the chance to add a new client to their books? Or perhaps the client is appealing, but the sticking point is the fee rate – the client wants a better deal. The firm doesn't want to lose the opportunity or turn away a keen client but is conflicted on price.

Conversely, the management may be tempted to take on work which seems lucrative but falls outside the firm's strategic parameters, at the risk that the content of the job will not to be attractive to the professionals required to do the work. This might occur if the task does not challenge the professionals' core competences, for example. Alternatively, professionals may want to develop their relationship with the client, only to find that managers disagree because of a strategic mismatch. Perhaps the project is too small or relatively unprofitable; nevertheless, the professionals involved find it an exciting assignment, because it represents something new and will give them a new a string to their bow.

Such dilemmas are unavoidable. The question is how firms deal with them, which may require case-by-case assessment, or a strong set of predefined guiding principles which team members can draw on in less certain scenarios.

Operational improvement consulting firm Trinity Horne is clear about its focus, as Managing Director Brendan Cahill explains:

> Our goal is to deliver measurable increases in our clients' productivity, particularly where client-facing and front-line management is concerned. We want the market to recognize that's our core area of expertise so our challenge is to invest in areas and tools that reinforce this, both in terms of the consulting process and our external image.

One recent example has been to build skills in mathematical and computer modeling, enabling the firm to take a far more explicitly fact-based approach to solving complex operational problems. But this approach has also required a clearer understanding of what the firm will *not* do:

> If we want clients to recognize us for our strengths, we need to reciprocate by being consistent. If one of our clients asked us to implement a big IT system, simply because they knew and liked us, we'd have to say no, because that's not our core area of expertise. We have to stay true to what we're good at – Brendan Cahill, Trinity Horne.

KPMG, a provider of audit, tax, and advisory services in the UK and globally, is another firm which remains true to its core strategy, despite operating in a ferociously competitive market:

> Client service is at the heart of what we do; if we get the client service right in every way the profitability should follow. We're highly selective: we try to avoid compliance work but focus on more specialized, added-value services. If you take everything that's offered, you can seem a bit desperate – top executive at KPMG.

For KPMG, it is not only for its own sake, but for the perception of its clients that it has decided to stick to what it is good at and what it is known for, particularly as clients have become more discriminating: 'Being one of the "Big Four" means we can tick all sorts of boxes, but we underestimate how much our clients segment us in terms of what we're good at, and what we're not so good at', the KPMG executive goes on to note.

Saying no to easy money can be one of the hardest challenges of all, especially when market conditions are tough and new business is hard to come by. However, if knowledge-intensive firms fail to prioritize in accordance with their chosen strategy, there *is* no strategy – above and beyond making money on everything that moves. If good intentions slip in this way, it is dangerous to promote a strategy of being the best in a particular field, providing a superior service or particularly in-depth consulting, or serving a certain client segment.

Without a strategy governing the choice of assignments and clients, a firm will develop in an ad-hoc, opportunistic way, based on the short-term maximization of assignments. A further risk associated with this is that it provides no opportunity for strategic recruitment, leverage, strategic client development, or skills acquisition. The result will be decisions that do not sufficiently support the desire of the best professionals for professional development and strong management – in other words, strategic direction. At the same time, clients are quickly likely to lose respect for a knowledge-intensive firm with a free-floating strategy.

Remaining strong in a tough market

Defining and following a strategy means being selective – deciding what the firm will and won't do to get to where it wants to be. Such choices consolidate the company strategy.

Any deviation from strategy, then, must be considered carefully, with full awareness of the risks as well as the potential gains.

Tony Tiernan, formerly responsible for marketing at the Boston Consulting Group in Europe and globally, now runs his own firm, Authentic Identity, based near Boston, Massachusetts. He has strong views on the consequences of being seduced by business opportunities that do not conform to company strategy:

> In tough times, many professional firms revert to two tactics that appear essential but actually dig them deeper in the hole both during and after a downturn. The first is selling work at which they cannot be truly great, and the second is pursuing clients that do not share their values.

Both tactics can help fill the short-term revenue void. But the consequences can be severe: unhappy clients who will not come back, a damaged reputation in the marketplace, and disaffected staff who will leave at the first opportunity. All of these chickens will come home to roost when the upturn comes, as it will.

The pressures to make these compromises are certainly understandable. But they can irreparably damage a consulting firm's core value-creating identity – the often unwritten principles about what the firm does (the business problems it chooses to own and solve) and the way it operates (the meaning and purpose that drives its business – the difference it is trying to make in the world – and the values that shape its relationships with clients and staff).

A consulting firm that does the hard work of discovering and articulating its identity can use it as a tool to shape the firm's three core business processes: developing clients; developing people; and developing ideas. The result is an organization that is 'all of a piece' – inherently differentiated and coherent while retaining the flexibility that professionals value. That is the foundation for a powerful professional services brand.

From a long-term strategic perspective, a lack of work does not justify a knowledge-intensive firm pursuing assignments in other markets than those where it has been strategically decided that the firm should operate.

If, for example, a highly reputed firm offering extensively customized services and high levels of client interaction at high fees takes on low-touch assignments with low customization requirements at low fees just to keep its professionals occupied, clients will soon discover that the firm is prepared to undertake more standardized work, and/or that it is moveable on pricing. As a result, the strategic identity of the knowledge-intensive firm will be destabilized. Professionals will also be frustrated, as they are not being given the chance to apply their skills and experience in a sufficiently focussed way. Being associated with a type of solution they were not originally recruited for may also lead to personal frustration. Additionally, it is expensive to delegate work to overqualified professionals.

At the other extreme, a knowledge-intensive firm normally engaged in low customization and low client interaction markets would be unwise to take on assignments demanding high levels of customization and client interaction, soon finding themselves challenged on strategic identity. Moreover, the application of resources will not be efficient, since professionals will need to put in too many hours to deliver the service – which still may not live up to the quality expected by the client.

In both cases, it would be strategically more advantageous to the knowledge-intensive firm to spend any 'downtime' applying spare resources to market and client development activities. It takes a long time to establish a strategic identity that might be destroyed overnight by a few mistakes and misplaced signals.

Resisting market pressure

As sound as these arguments might seem, a great number of knowledge-intensive firms find it difficult to stick to their strategy and execute it consistently. Some learn and improve. Others flow with the market and lose their edge.

Danish strategic communications firm, Masters Kommunikation, has a clear strategic understanding of its position and its preferred market. In more recent years, the company has changed its portfolio from ordinary PR services to strategic communication. Søren Schnedler, the owner and founder, recalls the firm's first years after a management buy-out following disagreements on strategy, after which Schnedler decided to follow a new path:

> I fired clients, I hired people, etc. It was tough, a new firm, all running on borrowed capital, and the IT bubble was beginning to burst. However, I did all those things. I have been true to my choice. We must be the best at what we do. Of course it is difficult. When we were down, we accepted small assignments, the low-hanging fruit, to put food on the table. But in general we are true to our strategy, more now than ever.

Strategic priorities are just as important in an organization in the public sector as in a private company, as Agnete Gersing, Director of the Danish Competition Authority, comments:

> We need to be extremely careful about how we prioritize our resources. In the spring, we had a major case on which we spent 10,000 hours. It is crucial that, given our framework, we select the cases which have the greatest impact. That is a challenge to us as an organization. Even if we try to be very conscientious when prioritizing major projects, we still spend a lot of time on smaller issues, which engender no strategic profit. We have to undertake a thorough assessment in order to identify the most important case strategically. The challenge is to minimize the amount of time spent on issues of low strategic importance.

So how does the Authority achieve this?

> We have strategy meetings with the management where we discuss whether we should continue to work on a given case. In those meetings, we then give priority to the cases that maximum potential. However, we must also take on reported cases. Other cases we take on because they are important in relation to our principles.
>
> We have a diagram which helps us to focus on, among other things, how large is the industry? Will we make decisions on the basis of principles? What level of resource consumption is expected? Then, as a logical extension, we assess whether the task adds up in terms of resources. We have some very clear criteria that apply when we take on projects. We also have transparent communication, so staff are able to understand why we have chosen not to proceed with a particular project. The whole process is based on decisions made at management level.

Quality decisions

When establishing its strategy, the knowledge-intensive firm must determine the desired level of quality of the services to be delivered, from three generally accepted categories:

- Excellent quality every time – high fee market.
- Generally high quality – middle fee market.
- Good enough quality – low fee market.

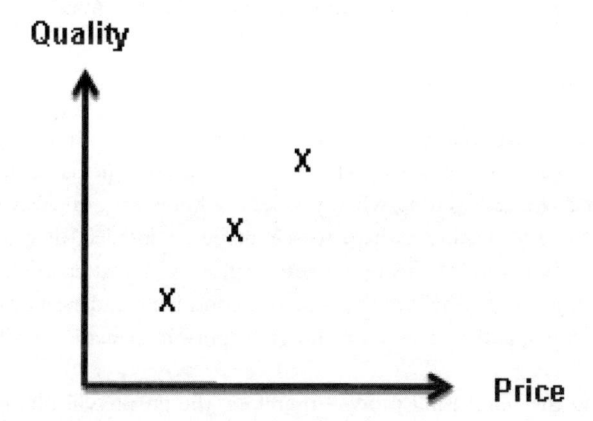

FIGURE 4.2 In knowledge-intensive firms, quality and price are closely associated

The quality level is a strategic issue because price and quality are closely associated, to the point that clients often use price as a guide to the level of quality they can expect (Figure 4.2). For this reason, in addition to being a competitive parameter in itself, price is also a signal of the firm's credentials and status to its target market. This is because pricing typically reflects the resources allocated to an assignment. On the basis that 'you get what you pay for', clients seeking top quality will be expecting to pay a premium to gain access to the talent and experience they require. Similarly, the price will also reflect the investment made by the firm in employing, retaining, and developing suitably qualified professionals.

An ambition to supply high quality every time can be fulfilled only through the conscious choice to *deliver* high quality every time. Without the investment to enable this follow-through, firms should resist promising the world to their clients, as they will only disappoint.

If, however, they have made this active and conscious choice of delivering the uppermost quality level, the knowledge-intensive firm must apply the same high standards when consolidating its recruitment, development, sales, and delivery strategy. If the quality level is less than excellent or fluctuates, word will soon get around, undermining any reputation the firm has tried to build based on its best assignments. The firm's strategic identity will be compromised, as clients won't know what to expect from the firm.

Signals confirming the firm's chosen quality parameters will include instances where the firm declines assignments because the management has concluded that it will not be possible to deliver the high levels of quality the company is known for.

In this way, strategy is seen to be executed simply by turning down work. Anyone can say yes, but not everyone is able to say no.

Managing expectations

Matching the expectations of the firm and its clients is a critical factor in achieving – and in being seen to achieve – success. Clients do not always know what they are getting when purchasing knowledge-intensive services, because the end product is hard to see, being an intellect-driven piece of work. A major part of the purchasing process is a matter of confidence, then: do I, as a client, believe that you as a consultant understands my needs and challenges, and that you are the right person to help me achieve my goals?

During the purchasing process, therefore, the client will often draw on others' experiences of knowledge-intensive firms to determine who has a track record for delivering according to client expectations.

For the knowledge-intensive firm, building a good reputation is essential to support the sales process. This means delighting rather than disappointing clients, and fulfilling their expectations.

This is an important point. A good reputation is not constructed by delivering excellent quality alone. If the quality has been superior but the result doesn't meet the client's expectations, that premium work will have been wasted. On the other hand, a good reputation can be established by providing services on a level *below* the best quality in the market among clients who are not looking for a top-of-the-range solution but, rather, the 'best fit'.

Ultimately, a reputation is built through the consistent fulfillment of client expectations of a given level of quality *and how this is used to achieve a required result*. To ensure this, the knowledge-intensive firm must design and harness its strategy and business model to deliver the service required by its target clients, in such a way that it meets the client's expectations first and foremost. There is no point in the supplier being proud of the finished job if the client is not.

The pursuit of excellence

Although the definition of 'excellence' is subjective, knowledge-intensive firms seen to deliver it will have a competitive edge. Success breeds success. Figure 4.3 illustrates the connection between client loyalty and professionals' credentials.

By delivering excellence and thereby creating high client satisfaction every time, a firm develops momentum. The value chain of a knowledge-intensive firm's strategy of excellence is illustrated in Figure 4.4: the value chain unites the loyalty of clients and professionals respectively, creating the foundation of a lucrative business in terms of profits and excellence.

There are two important, self-perpetuating developments at play here. First, satisfied clients become loyal clients, and satisfied, loyal clients are willing to pay high fees for excellence. This creates solid profitability in the knowledge-intensive firm, enabling further investment to be made in the development of professionals' competences and in the development of methodologies and solutions.

Secondly, satisfied clients will award their most difficult and challenging assignments to the knowledge-intensive firms they are most satisfied with. Thus, professionals in these firms tend to get the most challenging tasks, keeping them keen and further embellishing their skill sets and breadth of marketable experience. This results in satisfied professionals, making it

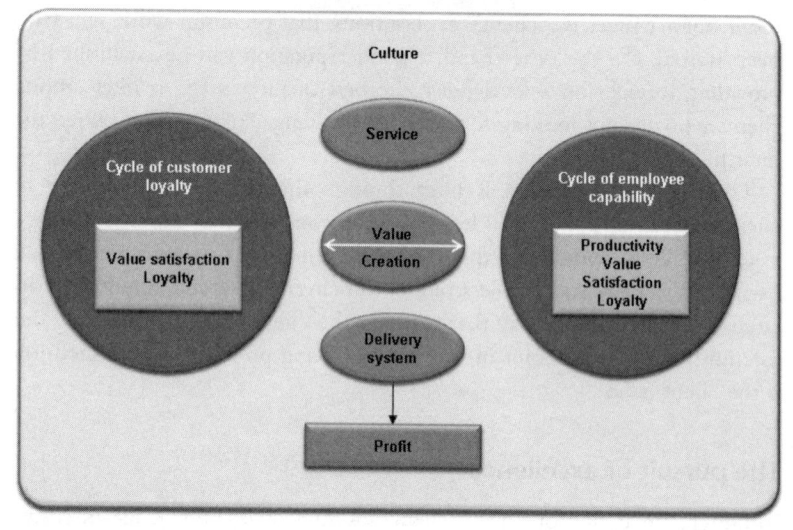

FIGURE 4.3 The value of employee competence and client loyalty
Source: Heskett *et al.* (1997)

possible for the firm to attract and retain the best professionals, who in turn form the core assets of the business.

Anders Lavesen, partner at leading Scandinavian law firm Kromann Reumert, has this to say about the significance of pursuing a reputation for delivering excellent quality:

> It is essential for us to be recognized as the best player in the field and having high profits. Without high profits we would not be able to maintain a position where we are among the very best. Quite simply, we could not retain top-notch partners and professionals. Career opportunities, being a good lawyer and a well-paid one as well, combined with a high professional level with stimulating clients and colleagues – that is a positive spiral.

Kromann Reumert's vision is simple: 'We set the standard'.

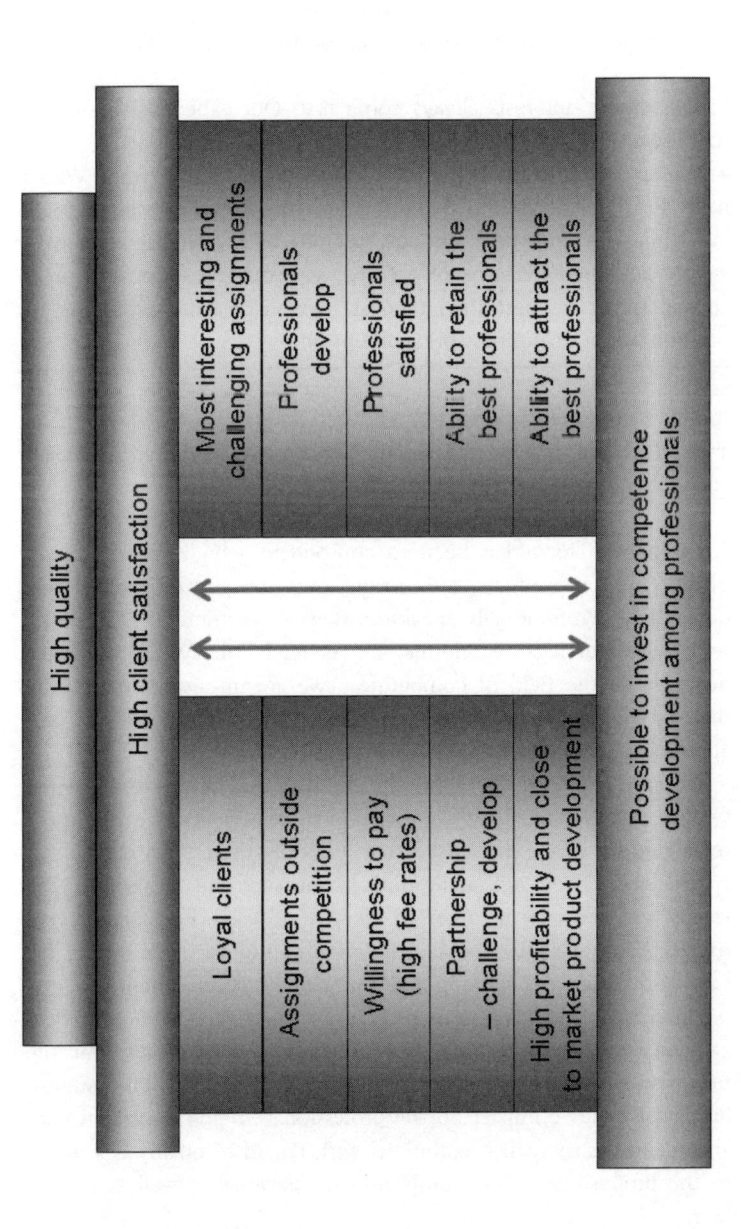

FIGURE 4.4 The value chain of knowledge-intensive firms

> American investment bank Goldmann Sachs clearly puts excellence at the center of its strategy, where its clients are the primary focus. These are among the business principles set out on the firm's website:
>
> > 1: Our clients' interests always come first. Our experience shows that if we serve our clients well, our own success will follow.
> > 4: We take great pride in the professional quality of our work. We have an uncompromising determination to achieve excellence in everything we undertake. Though we may be involved in a wide variety and heavy volume of activity, we would, if it came to a choice, rather be best than biggest. (www2.goldmansachs.com/our-firm/about-us/business-principles.html)

In the public sector, the Danish Competition Authority also prides itself on the pursuit of excellence. Director Agnete Gersing explains what this means in practice from a public sector perspective:

> An important focus has been to consolidate a high and consistent quality in our products. The assignments we get are exceedingly demanding. Professionally speaking, they are extremely challenging with regard to legal, economic, and general skills. When we make decisions in the field of competition, we are up against companies that have access to unlimited resources, hire the best lawyers, and appeal all the way to the Supreme Court.
>
> We have standards that define quality. The difficulty is to see when we live up to them. This is a question of experience. We have peer reviewing by very experienced staff, typically those who handle our appeal cases. Their task is to find all mistakes and weaknesses. We rectify and run tests in order to identify mistakes. Furthermore, we have ongoing dialogue about quality and consolidation of quality. We have also designed a training and competence development program on the basis of our strategy work.
>
> Some employees feel the process is somewhat heavy, but the majority by far confirms that the quality has improved. The progress has had a positive impact on the professionals. Being associated with an organization which is ambitious with regard to quality is a bonus to the professional who is ambitious on personal as well as societal levels.

We have some key indicators on which we perform a systematic follow-up. We have launched a new strategy in competence development with a new system to train people faster. We now have better, more systematic knowledge-sharing, experience groups, a new intranet, and 'lesson learned' projects. We focus on consolidating the knowledge we have and applying it systematically. We have changed our salary system in order to be able to reward the best of our professionals. We have a new recruitment policy, and a new strategy with regard to job vacancies.

Practicing excellence

It is easy to specify a strategy for excellence. Consolidating it in daily decisions is difficult, however. This demands great dedication on the part of the knowledge-intensive firm and its management. Those who aim for the top will face considerable challenges. They will need to make huge commitments to quality at every level of the organization, from procedures to the credentials and behavior of every single employee and manager.

Clearly, the pursuit of excellence must be the guiding principle of the organization, whether in terms of recruiting the best people, developing professionals, client handling, staff measuring systems, incentives structures – and sanction policies.

It is unlikely, then, that knowledge-intensive firms will find themselves in the 'excellence' category by accident, even if they believe the quality of their work meets the highest standards. Unless they have made the pursuit of excellence a fundamental strategic choice, upon which all decisions are based, they cannot and should not aim to play in this field.

Maintaining standards

Choices are necessary. Not just at the outset, but repeatedly. The demand for quality is continually challenged by the market: by the fees the client is prepared to pay; by the layout of the service; the delivery process; the time allocated to produce it; the types of materials and tools to be applied in solutions; and in recruitment. This is where strategic action is expressed – in the choices made by the knowledge-intensive firm when it takes on assignments and selects methods of delivery.

A strategy of excellence requires that professionals are always able to see the strategy implemented through their actions. Only in this way will excellence proliferate culturally in the organization as a value to be respected.

This means the management must take the lead in implementing high performance and consistent excellence. This can be done via the cultural modeling of professionals through value management and dialog to instill among professionals the preferred values that must guide direct actions.

Knowledge-intensive firms with a focus on excellence must carefully consider which type of clients they prefer and are prepared to work for.

On occasion, managers will needs to remind professionals of the level of excellence required and what it takes to achieve the goal. They, too, must execute strategically in all actions, where necessary imposing sanctions on professionals who fail to meet the required standard.

Ultimately, a professional may have to leave the firm if their actions are deemed unacceptable, potentially detracting from the brand identity the firm is striving to maintain.

When 'good enough' will do

Plenty of knowledge-intensive firms operate successfully outside the 'excellence' market, demonstrating that there is a demand for a less-than-blue-chip service. Although most clients may believe that they are looking for excellence, many do not want to pay the high fees this demands. Other clients, when it comes down to it, do not actually need excellence. These two factors are often connected.

Knowledge-intensive firms *not* striving to over-perform may differentiate themselves via other factors than excellence. Differentiation may be on the basis of 'good enough' quality coupled with speed of delivery and/or competitive pricing. The important thing here is to be strategically *conscious* of what they are providing so that this matches the expectations of the client. They will also need to guard against being compared unfavorably with either players in the 'excellence' bracket or those in a lower market category, where pricing is even lower.

Managing expectations will be particularly important if there may be variations in standards across different activities or scenarios where specialist resources are unavailable for a given assignment. Clients must know what they are paying for and what they will get. If their expectations are met, the client will be happy and the fees will seem justified.

Clearly, professionals must be recruited and retained on a level corresponding to the service the organization is aiming to deliver, and to the quality level preferred by the firm.

American-Canadian consulting firm International Profit Associates (IPA) has established itself in a market advising small businesses with a turnover of $0.5–10 million on company development and optimization. The firm is strongly standardized, providing business analysis for clients according to a systematic concept which does not vary much from client to client. The company prides itself on the value of the services it provides but, in keeping with its target client base positions, these as affordable rather than top of the range.

IPA's services are cheaper than those offered by more well-known consulting firms; they have to be, otherwise the client base of small companies would not buy IPA. The most important profit driver is obviously utilization in a continuous add-on sales program: employees' working days are planned efficiently to ensure a comprehensive resource allocation.

Agents call businesses to sell two-day diagnostic studies to be performed by business analysts located all over the US at a price of $350. In 2003 hundreds of phoners generated 1,400 studies a day, 80 percent of which actually were conducted. Agents are paid by study conducted to incentivize serious client relations.

The day after the business agrees with the agent to have the study, the business analyst visits the business for the two-day standard diagnostic study leading to suggestions for optimization measures, often including also the suggestion of a more in-depth survey of the business at an average of $890 which is acquired by approximately 25 percent of diagnosed businesses.

Approximately 25 percent of surveyed businesses end up also buying consulting priced at $195 an hour for at least 100 hours. The IPA business model has proven very successful (see Figure 4.5).

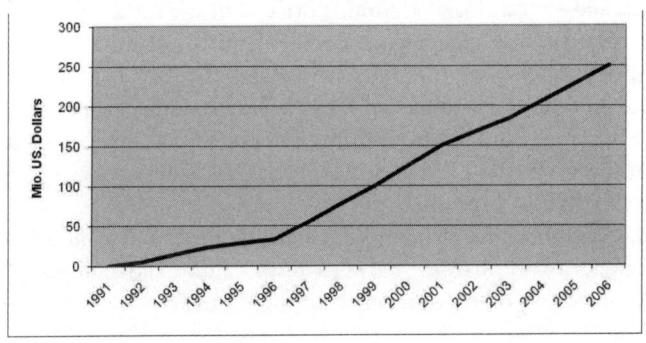

FIGURE 4.5 IPA's turnover
Note: the turnovers in 1992, 1994, 1996, 1999, 2001, 2003 and 2006 are gleaned from IPA's homepage (http://www.ipa-c.com/about–us/milestones.asp). The turnovers of the remaining years are listed as averages. The most recently published figures are from 2006

> Clarifying where IPA sits in the market, the company's website adds:
>
>> No company wants to find itself lacking adequate cash flow ... or in a disjointed organization. As a result, many companies are re-evaluating their funding requirements, predetermining their profit margin and rethinking their overall business strategy. Those are the three most popular reasons that small and medium-size business owners invite IPA and IBA into their business. From the initial introduction of IPA by our sales representative, to the diagnostic business analysis, to a full-service consulting engagement, our clients receive maximum value and benefit delivered by professionals. (www.ipa-c.com/)

By finding the right business model and communicating the value proposition for the market, knowledge-intensive firms can establish and develop a good business, however they position themselves in the quality league.

Poor positioning and planning is the real risk – not the chosen market. Decide where your focus is and you'll be able to go after the right staff, and the right clients. Without that direction, bad choices and poor progress will be made.

Price wars

Firms choosing to operate on a medium-quality level, competing primarily on price to appeal to a broad client base, may find they have a larger market to play for but, again, will need to get their business model right to ensure that they (1) meet client expectations, so that they get repeat business and referrals; and (2) can make a profit if price is their primary lever.

Recruitment and competence development in this case must be based on professional profiles matching market needs. They may look for staff who are professionally strong and find the business model appealing, and are so able to develop ambitions to realize the potential of strategy of the firm, or generalists who are good at delivering precisely the services and products which this type of firm offers.

Salary and incentive structures must match the business model, too. The same applies to the balance between team culture and individual culture, and the matching of expectations with those of clients.

Summary

In this chapter, we have seen how a strategy can be rendered worthless if it is not applied systematically to everyday operations, including decisions about when and how business is chosen or rejected.

By failing to execute its strategy and to reinforce their strategic identity (clients' perception of the firm), there is a risk that firms are leaving strategic decisions to the whims of market. While it may seem financially beneficial to take the opportunist stance and flow with the market, this can create confusion among clients and professionals, undermining the brand values the firm may have worked hard to build.

As we have seen, a knowledge-intensive firm will define its strategy through the choices of what it does *not* do, as well as what it *does* do. The knowledge-intensive firm must prioritize and invest its resources in accordance with the strategic focus. Although this is particularly true for private firms, public organizations too must prioritize resources when selecting assignments and prioritizing work.

We have also challenged the myth by which more or less all knowledge-intensive firms attempt to market themselves: that they deliver excellence. Our belief is that it is perfectly valid to deliver solutions and services that are adequate or very good, without the need for a five-star rating – indeed, that there are plenty of knowledge-intensive firms successfully doing this, and plenty of clients who actively seek out this level of service. Delivering excellence every time is excessively demanding and only a fraction of companies in the market have the ability and not least the dedication to do so; at the same time, not many clients are able or willing to pay it.

As we have discussed, it is more important for managers to know what type of market the firm operates in so that they can execute the strategy appropriately to create a successful business. Provided the firm meets its clients' expectations, concerns about quality levels can be restricted to those which apply only in the world in which they have chosen to operate.

Questions for reflection

- Do you often refrain from taking on assignments because they do not fall within the scope of your firm's strategy?
- How do you manage the relationship between pricing and quality in your firm?
- How do you ensure client loyalty as well as employee loyalty?
- Where would you position your firm on a scale from 1 to 10 (where 1 = inferior and 10 = superior) in terms of its ability to take conclusive action, following a failure to deliver the desired quality level?

5
EMPLOYEE CAPITAL

In this chapter, we take a closer look at the employees and, specifically, at the professionals – the talent – of knowledge-intensive firms, given that they constitute the most valuable assets of this type of firm. We consider the type of professionals firms employ, their skills and experience profiles, the means by which competences can be developed, and the importance of acknowledging and responding to professionals' ambitions and preferences (Figure 5.1).

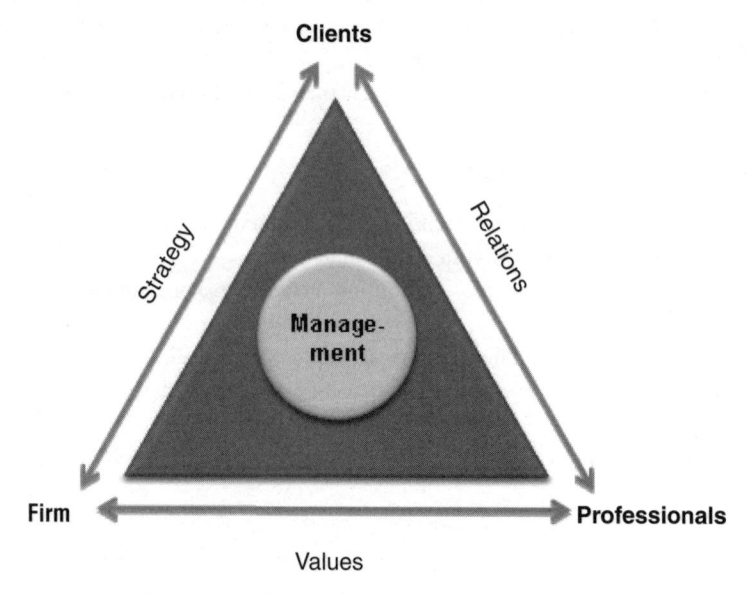

FIGURE 5.1 Employees in the knowledge-intensive firm

As we have noted from the outset, in knowledge-intensive firms it is the professional individuals themselves who make up a large part of the 'solution' being offered to clients. Without them, there would be no business or service. Their skills, performance, and satisfaction levels are therefore paramount.

As American business management guru and writer Tom Peters (2006) puts it, 'A PSF [professional service firm] adds value through one and only one thing: the accumulation of creative intellectual capital'. Indeed, professionals are a crucial driver in the firm's ability to deliver quality results, client satisfaction, profits, and onward development. Taking this to its logical conclusion, Lorsch and Tierney, authors of *Aligning the Stars* (2002), believe that, in the case of the knowledge-intensive firm, 'The people you pay are more important over time than the people who pay you'.

In a chicken-and-egg scenario, a knowledge-intensive firm would never get off the ground without the professionals to deliver the solution, so a strategy that puts the demands of the client first, at the detriment of the needs of its core employees, is risky. In the longer term, if the quality, experience, and fulfillment of the firm's professionals are maintained and developed, clients will keep coming back and the business will grow. If, on the other hand, professionals grow frustrated and leave – perhaps because they are being assigned to the wrong projects or their skills and career development is being neglected – the result could be the loss of hard-won client relationships as clients leave with them or do not stay as loyal to the firm as before.

This applies even if 'profit' is removed from the equation, with consequences for knowledge-intensive firms in the public as well as the private sector. As the following comments from the Managing Director of the Danish Competition Authority, Agnete Gersing, show, the approach to valuing and prioritizing the needs of professionals is just as strong outside the commercial environment:

> We work with strategy charts. The essential pillar is the employees who are extremely important in our organization. We live by our employees and the knowledge that is contained in their heads. Thus, a very important part of our strategy is how to recruit, retain, and develop our employees; for this, we have a management development and competence development strategy.

Management by presence and absence

After many years in management and management-related research, it is our experience that professionals in knowledge-intensive firms have particular demands in terms of their working life, job content, and professional and personal development. Driven to excel in their fields, they are likely to crave challenges, opportunities to develop or try something new, responsibility, excitement, and meaning. In short, professionals are very demanding in terms of what their work should offer them – not just with regard to salary, but also when it comes to development and perceived status.

The ultimate challenge to managers in knowledge-intensive firms is to fulfill the individual demands of each professional, while striking the right balance between visible (hands-on) and light-touch (absence of) management. For example, professionals will want a certain level of independence and the room to shine, yet while still receiving attention and feedback so that they feel appreciated and that they are on a development path that will fulfill their personal and professional ambitions. This is essential to keep them interested and to keep their skills fresh and current. Getting the balance right is not easy, especially as needs may vary for each individual and according to where that professional is in their career and role at the current organization.

While the successful handling of professionals will also rely on the manager's ability to read and understand each individual's character and unique set of needs, they must also have a firm grasp of their own role in the process of inspiring and nurturing professionals so that they stay with, and perform well for, the firm for the optimum length of time. It could be argued that this last dimension has not been given sufficient priority in management research to date.

Most managers of professionals originate from within the profession. Knowledge-based strategy researchers Sveiby and Lloyd (1987) describe the attitude that has prevailed for many years: 'It is impossible to lead professionals without being a professional yourself.' In our view, this assumption is not quite accurate, but in many knowledge-intensive firms it has become a benchmark for best practice – that the most important quality for a leader of other professionals is that they have been at the coal-face themselves.

Examples are abundant: managing partners in law firms, consulting firms, engineering firms, and accounting firms are often recruited internally – i.e. managers have grown up within the firm, where their primary skills will have been operational in nature. When a management position becomes available, the best/most senior consultant, lawyer, accountant, or engineer is promoted, and an assumption is made that this person will be capable of managing other professionals. The same thing occurs frequently in the public sector. Here, the lawyer or the economist with the best professional qualifications is appointed manager. In hospitals, many doctors are placed in management positions despite having no management credentials. The same goes for deans and other management positions at universities.

Professionals are expected to be able to manage professionals and, perhaps by osmosis, master what is required – the ability to inspire and create enthusiasm, and to foster a culture of feedback and team spirit. In reality, however, internal ladder-climbing rarely automatically qualifies someone to become a manager. Whatever their professional experience and credentials, assuming the role of manager and leader will require a new and quite different set of skills if the firm is to continue to progress.

Without ensuring that these qualities exist in a manager, the prognosis is simple and predictable. Poor decisions will be made, professionals' personal development may stall, and morale will suffer. Regrettably, this has been the experience of a wide range of knowledge-intensive firms.

Managing professionals is not simply a case of assigning them to and directing them in a task, as we have already noted. Professionals also need to be challenged and incentivized in special ways, which again demands certain skills from the manager. The professionally well founded expert, the prima donna, and the person with the super-ego, will have a burning need for goals and direction. If these are not met, the risk is that they will look elsewhere for the challenges they need to grow.

In the meantime, the quality of their work could suffer. Recent research has shown that the ability to progress is the top motivator affecting professionals' performance:

> On days when workers have the sense they're making headway in their jobs, or when they receive support to overcome obstacles, their emotions are most positive and their drive to succeed is at its peak. On days when they feel they are spinning their wheels or encountering roadblocks to meaningful accomplishment, their mood and motivation are lowest. (Amabile and Kramer, 2010)

Fortunately, the need for managers to have a special skill set outside their operational credentials is now being increasingly recognized. As a result, knowledge-intensive firms across both the private and public sector can be seen rolling out or strengthening management training programs, with a view to boosting the managerial capacity of the company. In many cases, this is the only way forward, since good managers with relevant market-specific knowledge are hard to find on the open market.

The following five approaches are important elements in a manager's repertoire:

1. An awareness of what makes the professional employee tick. This is the main driver of motivation, so understanding and empathy are important preconditions for managing these individuals.
2. The foresight to formulate new occupational challenges and definite goals through a dialog between manager and professional. It is by such measures that the professional makes progress from a personal and a career perspective.
3. A readiness to provide continuous support and nurturing, including encouragement and feedback. This is very important even for highly skilled professionals.
4. The ability to implement management in ways that promote and maximize self-management.
5. Managerial qualifications.

Beyond remuneration: rewarding professionals

As we have indicated, salary is not the only tool by which managers can be seen to appreciate and acknowledge the performance of professionals. Delegating challenging assignments with developmental potential is a significant tool for signaling appreciation. Acknowledgement can also be given through constructive feedback – which should include praise as well as a deconstruction of weak performances and how these can be improved – plus proactive development and coaching.

Another way of compensating professionals for their hard work is through customized 'treats' created with the individual in mind – whether an all-expenses-paid dinner with their spouse or partner in one of the better restaurants in town; a family weekend away; or the latest gadget or communications technology. The value needn't be high; the thought and gesture alone will go a long way.

Massaging egos

As already discussed, in knowledge-intensive firms value is created by the people responsible for performing assignments. The strengths and competences of the team have a direct bearing on quality and client satisfaction. Strong professionals are therefore the distinguishing characteristic differentiating many knowledge-intensive firms from their competitors.

Taking the lead in the market means being able to attract, retain, and field the best professionals available. Happily, these will typically be the professionals that demand the most challenging and exciting clients, because they will strive to gain the most from these engagements. The challenge here is to seek out the right kind of projects and to allocate assignments strategically, so that, as far as possible, these provide sustained opportunities for employee development, stimulation, and inspiration, exchange of knowledge and experience, and the chance for individuals to assume considerable responsibility – enabling them to shine.

Managing the ambitions of professionals involves another challenge which will be familiar to many managers, regardless of whether they operate in the private or public sector. The fact that the deployment of top experts, and the quality of the work they want to deliver, may involve greater resources than is economically justifiable, increasing the client's fees considerably. This issue can be particularly pronounced in the public sector where resource and budget management are often under great pressure.

Says Peter Høier, Director of the Competence Center at the Ministry of Foreign Affairs, in Denmark UMKC:

> I manage our projects by tracking the number of hours we spend on them. We might for instance allocate 50 hours to a certain task. Halfway through the project, we evaluate on time consumption to see if more hours are required. We may also conclude that the product will not get any better. The manager's statement: 'Friends, it just doesn't get any better' is a difficult issue for professionals. If you spent double the amount of time, the quality would not be twice as good, but only 5 percent better. Sometimes I do not want to pay that much more for the extra quality, because it is just good enough.
>
> It is precisely the same in a center like ours, and in other departments and public organizations as in the private sector. Being good at managing resources in my organization is one of the most important challenges I face as the director. It is tremendously difficult.

Agnete Gersing, Director at the Danish Competition Authority, adds:

> In recent years, we have preached quality, quality, quality, and quite deliberately avoided any mention of efficiency. You cannot stress both, because then you run the risk that nothing whatsoever happens. Now we must consolidate the high quality and maintain it. Then we will look at efficiency in order to reach a high performance level.

Not all solutions need to get top marks. Some of them would demand disproportionate amounts of resources to reach a level of excellence. Issues of minor strategic importance must be dealt with as quickly as possible with an acceptable quality.

However, the 50 percent extra resources spent to achieve 5 percent extra quality could be a good trade-off on strategically important tasks. Sometimes it is obvious where you should focus your resources. In other cases it might be more difficult. In those situations you have to be quite clear on priorities. We occasionally use the timeframe as a benchmark for quality, since quality is difficult to translate into operational issues. So we can say: 'Now you have 10 hours'. Many tasks can be solved in two hours or thirty hours, so we need to give direction.

Bringing on junior professionals

Because the services of a knowledge-intensive firm are often intangible, it is difficult to document the quality of the service in advance, which means the client doesn't always know in advance what they will get. Although the firm may have all the capabilities to deliver a truly excellent delivery, this will depend on the availability of the required resources and the budget and timescale allocated.

The challenge to the knowledge-intensive firm will be to ensure that professionals are not only competent and motivated, but also that they have the time to deliver the quality required. This demands flexibility and adaptability in the way resources are allocated.

Whether or not the knowledge-intensive firm has one or more professionals, and one or more clients, the ability to complete any assignment will determine the quality of the delivered solution. Clients often expect that the knowledge-intensive firm is capable of working and delivering within very tight timescales. Having hired an external supplier to assist with services needed, and paying a relatively high price for the privilege, they expect to get high-priority treatment.

They may therefore expect the highest expertise, demanding that only senior professionals with good CVs and experience work on their account. However, in order to ensure flexibility, knowledge-intensive firms need to be able to field other professionals, perhaps including more junior staff.

Understandably, younger professionals will often be least in demand, since they are less well known in the market and may be deemed inexperienced and liable to make mistakes. Yet it is these employees which constitute the flexible staff of the knowledge-intensive firm, enabling the business to take on more work and spread its talent economically.

In order to be able to apply this flexibility, the firm will need to help its clients to accept the value that more junior employees bring to the table – for example keeping costs down, enabling pressing deadlines to be met, etc. Public sector knowledge-intensive firms are also familiar with the challenge of leveraging professionals to an optimal degree in assignments.

Says Agnete Gersing of the Danish Competition Authority:

> Training people is a significant driver of our success. Experience is important to us, since industry expertise demands experience, and as a relatively small organization we cover the entire economy. The less experience we have, the more problems we encounter. Competition law is complex, because to a great extent it is case law. You can read the law, but you must also know the cases and the concise rulings, the Danish competition law as well as the EU laws. The longer time you have been in the game, the better. We also realize that it will be unlikely to recruit younger people and retain them for 10–15 years. So we recruit younger as well as more experienced employees.

Recruiting the right people

If a knowledge-intensive firm is only as good as the people it employs, it follows that the right recruitment strategy and approach will be paramount. The best skills in any market will be the hardest to find – the higher up the ladder the position, the more difficult it will be to track down the right blend of skills and experience being sought.

In a 1989 analysis, consulting firm McKinsey & Company introduced the concept of 'the war for talent' (McKinsey & Company, 2001). In a competitive market, particularly where firms differentiate themselves based on the quality of their professionals, winning the talent war could mean winning the battle for market share.

Success doesn't come by accident. Nor can it be guaranteed by offering the highest salary (even where firms can afford this). According to McKinsey & Company's findings, the three most popular factors influencing talent attraction and retention are: a firm's values and culture; the scope for autonomy in the job; and good management.

Many knowledge-intensive firms apply 'employer branding' as a means of encapsulating the values of the firm and to send out a coherent message to potential recruits about the benefits of working there; just as, if not more importantly, this branding helps to ensure that firms attract the right professionals *in accordance with their company strategy*.

To maximize recruitment success, firms must commit themselves to creating the right reputation among target groups from which the firm primarily wants to attract personnel. Some firms focus primarily on hiring new graduates. In this model, the firm should establish a brand presence in universities and business schools to promote itself to students. McKinsey & Company has done this, having established prizes for the best papers in various training courses and inviting top-grade students from selected schools to dinner events and for travel offers. Consulting firm Accenture, meanwhile, has run huge campaigns with the world-renowned golfer Tiger Woods as the main attraction.

Other knowledge-intensive firms recruit primarily from among more experienced people and target their branding accordingly, stressing the advantages this target group of professionals will obtain by joining the firm.

Blanket targeting, or hiring the wrong people, can be costly because:

- the recruitment process takes time;
- induction, orientation and training take time;
- time and quality are lost in the services delivered, if there is a poor match;
- phasing out the person who turns out not to be right for the firm is also time-consuming; and
- it is delegitimizing for a manager to hire the wrong people, indicating that the manager is somehow lacking professionally.

For these reasons, many firms spend time conducting multiple rounds of interviews and assessment sessions, where different managers have a chance to meet candidates – and the chance to discuss their suitability with other managers from elsewhere in the firm. Another common practice is to apply external resources in the recruitment process, as well as various types of tests. The greater the certainty the organization can reach in determining whether a candidate is the right person for the job at the outset, the better for the business in the long term.

Retention through continuous development

Once the selected professionals are on board, the development process must begin – to motivate professionals so that they remain interested and loyal, and to develop their market value.

Competence development

In knowledge-intensive firms, the best opportunity to develop professionals' skills takes place through active project work. Each assignment will present a new challenge, a chance to apply their knowledge in a slightly different way, a chance to learn and to add something new to their repertoire and experience bank.

Clearly, professionals need training and education too. Yet this must be consolidated in everyday practice by applying skills in real-time projects. This gives the professional the chance to cement the new knowledge and techniques they have acquired, building their confidence. Training courses in isolation can fail to fulfill, leaving professionals disappointed and demotivated and potentially leaving the firm out of pocket. Unless the content is quickly consolidated in everyday operational work, there is a good chance the training will turn out to have been a waste of time for all parties. Feeding any training into a fuller development program, on the other hand, will ensure, accelerate, and enhance the impact.

At the UK's Institute for Development Studies, Elizabeth Maddison explains that research projects are important not only in funding the Institute, but in developing the expertise of researchers:

> We start from quite a high base of specialized knowledge in that nearly all Fellows are appointed with a DPhil and in some cases, several years' post-doctoral experience. At the highest levels we're appointing some individuals who have had senior posts in internationally reputable universities and think tanks. Our other research and knowledge services' staff typically have Masters qualifications. Because we work in such a specialized area, there is a virtuous circle. One of the reasons why we'll win a particular research contract will be the quality, track record, and experience of the people who will work on it, and they will write the bid and negotiate the contract. Many have long-standing international individual reputations, others are forging their careers, but each project adds to their portfolio and expertise, and their fieldwork experience and exposure to other partners, for example. Working on the contract will further enhance the knowledge of the people involved, building their reputation as academics and strengthening our position when it comes to winning future work.
>
> Arguably a greater challenge for us is developing the skills of those who are earlier in their careers, where the need to generate the 180 target of funded activity is really very demanding. We're doing a lot of work at present to understand better the issues facing newer and

younger staff in particular and what we can do about it – unlike big consultancies for example, we tend not to have a pyramid structure with more junior staff directed on specific projects that are managed by a much smaller number of 'senior partner' equivalents. Our structure is very flat in comparison. But we are looking now at our career structure and whether we need to make some significant changes.

Other ways of helping individuals keep abreast and hopefully at the leading edge in their field is to encourage them to publish widely, including in internationally refereed journals, to attend conferences, and the usual mix of academic activities that run alongside research. We try to enable Fellows to do this as part of their 40 working days when they are not expected to be generating funded work. In some cases we're also able to support sabbaticals but not as extensively as Fellows generally would wish.

Finally, many of our Fellows will also tell you – quite genuinely – that it's the presence of large numbers of MA and DPhil students, many of whom are international and highly experienced professionally before they come to us, that keeps them up to date and challenged, in the best sense of the word.

We have quite a tough regime of Fellowship review that evaluates each Fellow's work every four years by a panel including external assessors and that's quite a high hurdle, encouraging Fellows to make sure their work has currency and impact and will be well regarded by their peers – career decisions therefore depend on this.

As the talent 'war' intensifies in mature and highly competitive markets, many knowledge-intensive firms have enhanced their development programs to include more formally structured practices. This has included the foundation of internal 'training academies', to ensure targeted competence development.

> McKinsey & Company sends out a strong message around this on its website, on pages targeted at potential new recruits:
>
> From day one, we are committed to furthering your personal and professional development. We are confident that there is no other place where you can achieve and grow as much in such a short period of time.
>
> At McKinsey, you will:

- Help shape industries and organizations working with top-tier clients
- Find opportunities to grow and learn quickly through constant coaching and feedback
- Join a network that you will be part of for the rest of your life
- Become a leader through the challenges you are presented with and the responsibility you get. (www.mckinsey.com/locations/Copenhagen/Your_Career.aspx)

A and B players

Identifying potential stars and nurturing them along their journey to 'stardom' is a very important management task within knowledge-intensive firms. Stars are future partners and managers – in line management or in other functions, including key account managers, sales managers, bid managers, project managers, team leaders, and methodology and market developers. Stars should be developed via the right challenges and development plans to ensure optimal development paths at a high pace, challenging them continuously.

Stars often demand a lot of management attention because they have high self-esteem and have high ambitions for themselves. They crave management attention in the form of recognition and praise, and as a source of reassurance that they are firmly on the radar for further advancement.

Thomas J. DeLong, John J. Gabarro, and Robert J. Lees, respected academics in the field of professional leadership and authors of the book *When Professionals Have to Lead* (2007), as well as numerous theses published in *Harvard Business Review*, write:

> Like world-class athletes, professionals have an almost insatiable need to know how they are doing: the more able they are, the keener their need. One highly-regarded mentor in a law firm reflected, 'For some of my best performers, I have to tell them how well they are doing on Monday and again on Thursday. No amount of feedback is enough'. (DeLong *et al.*, 2008)

DeLong and Vijayaraghavan (2003) urge that managers in knowledge-intensive firms do not forget the 'B-players'. While stars (A-players) and C-players – the professionals not currently meeting standards of the firm – each demand relatively intense management attention, B-players tend not to get high-priority attention. This is largely because they don't articulate their need for management attention as much as A-players and C-players do.

B-players are important to the knowledge-intensive firm, however, and should be neglected at the firm's peril. These are stable producers who skillfully, efficiently, and without fuss complete one assignment after the other. Despite this, managers tend to pay more attention to the self-promoting, attention-seeking stars at one extreme, and under-performers at the other.

Not everyone can be a star. In their article, DeLong et al. (2008) state that the distribution of professionals in a knowledge-intensive firm typically follows the pattern 20 percent A-players, 10 percent C-players, and 70 percent B-players.

Even in high-performing organizations, B-players constitute the backbone of the firm and contribute substantially to the business – across sales, direct project work, and the development of juniors. In the long run, these stalwarts may in fact turn out to be more important to the business than its stars, particularly if the firm becomes particularly adept at maximizing the deployment of B-players' strong, but not always well advertised competences. The simple difference between retaining B-players for six years instead of four can be seen to create a direct result on the bottom-line, particularly as they are not overly demanding of fanfare and fuss.

Team performance

Most knowledge-intensive firms depend on teamwork as humans do on oxygen. When a group of good people co-operate, critique each other, and develop their projects, the logical conclusion is that quality improves. Only in rare instances of pure individual work will great results follow over time. Assignments based on individual solutions are, as a rule, small and the growth potential limited. Strong knowledge-intensive firms based primarily on individual performance tend to be the exception rather than the rule.

'I was only able to do what I did because I was a team player', says Shelia Evans-Tranumn of her 16 successful years as Associate Commissioner in the US, during which she took the New York State school system to the highest heights, being honored several times by the George W. Bush administration:

> Lone rangers don't last long: you have to have a team culture that says 'we are in this together'. I built a strong team culture with my managers, and I had them build strong team cultures with the people who worked for them. It is critically important.

Firstly, no-one has all the ideas for success. Secondly, if people don't feel they're valued, they won't support your project with all their knowledge. Great teams constantly connect outside the work to each other and to others; they have fun; they are innovative.

Team performance is important because it creates development and synergy through knowledge transfer, reflection, and flexibility in performing assignments. This being the case, it is vital that a knowledge-intensive firm *rewards* teamwork.

If teamwork is policy but incentive schemes reward lone players, the policy is dishonest and does not support the achievement of success. It will only take the professionals a second to figure out what is actually rewarded and they will react accordingly. By rewarding individual performance, the message being sent out is that team efforts take second priority. This may lead to tactical and sub-optimizing behavior, with colleagues resorting to gate-keeping and attempting to secure promotion at the expense of other professionals. In a world that demands still more complex competences, and where transparency and knowledge-sharing are paramount, the knowledge-intensive firms supporting these virtues will be the winners of tomorrow.

As professional services firm KPMG knows well, while technical know-how is often associated with particular individuals, making things happen requires teamwork. Providing clients with solutions that match their unique circumstances requires working across the firm's internal boundaries:

> You've got the best brains coming in, looking at [the requirement] from every angle and they're all with you, trying to help you out. We had one proposal where we were concerned that we didn't know enough about the client but, when we put our team together, we suddenly realized that one person knew a bit about this, someone else knew a bit about that, and so on. Talk about confidence – it made such a difference! But it only happened because the whole team rallied around – top executive at KPMG.

There is also a *vertical* dimension to teamwork at KPMG – the ability of people of all grades to work together on the client's behalf:

> Sometimes you'll look around at a team dinner and think, heavens, I can't believe all these people have been involved. We'll deliver a job well within the time that we're allocated and the quality of the work will be fantastic. The client will be happy and we'll make money.

The KPMG executive adds:

> You feel so proud of your staff because it's they that are doing it. We partners and senior managers will take all the credit for it, but it isn't just us: it's the people on the ground who are delivering excellent service.

Integrity is ingrained: 'We have to have an ethical perspective on things; it's part of our everyday lives – even at the cost of economic advantage. We'll turn work away'.

Culture is sustained by recruiting people who clearly fit the KPMG mould, by the continuity of people who've been with the firm for many years and by the way in which senior people act as mentors for more junior staff:

> We look for people we feel we can do business with. Could I work with them, sit next to them, be happy to have them on my team? There's formal training, but it's nothing like just learning on the ground. I've had mentors, not in the formal sense, but people whom I respected enormously. They were very happy to help; they'd take me along to meetings so I could watch and learn. There are lots of partners who still do that.

There's also a clear sense of what's right and wrong in terms of behavior:

> If you speak to somebody in human resources, they'll tell you it's all about process: we've got a values charter; we've got mentors; we have appraisal systems. I'm sure these things contribute, but ultimately it comes down to looking at the people you work with and seeing how they are behaving: what do they get patted on the back for, or kicked up the backside for? I've seen people try to cut corners to get a great result, only for someone to come down on them like a ton of bricks and say, 'well, for your short-term gain, you've got this wrong.

Anders Lavesen, of Kromann Reumert, says his organization places similar value on teamwork:

> We have a friendly competition between colleagues: we are colleagues, we studied together at law school, etc. When appointing partners, it is an important criterion that you are good at co-operating. The

professionals are aware of this, so this creates a strong culture. You cannot advance if you are a 'lone wolf'. Knowledge-sharing means that if you do not give, you do not receive.

Performance reviews

Given that highly competent professionals are often the primary source of differentiation for a knowledge-intensive firm, it is essential to keep a check on quality by continuously measuring performance. This should include monitoring of each professional's performance, development, and potential. This may be done through assessments of assignment success and regular appraisals. It is essential, too, that professionals are given their chance to give feedback, particularly in relation to their job satisfaction.

Monitoring employee satisfaction can be done in several ways:

- Continual benchmarking of employee satisfaction (at least once every year). This can ensure evaluation of satisfaction, including the closest manager's ability to create development for the individual and the team.
- Monitoring whether or not managers consolidate employee development via performance reviews (at least once every year or even three to four times a year), individual development plans (annually or every six months), and necessary continual feedback on projects and assignments.
- Monitoring of whether or not the project managers consolidate employee development through feedback to the team members after every single assignment.

Examples of ranking-based statements used in questionnaires to measure employee satisfaction in knowledge-intensive firms are as follows:

- I have enough challenges in my job.
- I am very motivated in my job.
- I have reasonable influence over my work.
- My work contributes to the creation of value for clients.
- I know when I have done a good job.
- Normally I have a reasonable balance between my working and private life.
- I apply my knowledge and my skills in my work.
- My closest manager gives me sufficient feedback on my work.
- My closest manager motivates me to do my best.
- My closest manager has credibility.

- How satisfied are you with the follow-up on your most recent performance review?
- In my department we help and support each other.
- In my department we have clear goals.
- We have a shared responsibility in order to consolidate quality.
- I am aware of the firm's goals and strategy.
- I have confidence in the management's way of leading the firm.
- I am proud of being employed by the firm.

Research demonstrates that professionals given performance reviews and appraisals are more satisfied than professionals who are not subjected to this process. But this is only true where managers follow up afterwards. Where there are no consequences, professionals are typically *more* dissatisfied than professionals whose performance has not been formally assessed (Storch *et al.*, 2010).

Up-or-out culture

A number of knowledge-intensive firms claim to have a well defined 'up-or-out' culture, demanding the continuous development and improvement of their employees: if this is found to be lacking, the professional concerned is eased out of the firm. In practise, claims of such a culture are rarely borne out, but the approach can have its merits – if only in focussing the organization on the importance of progression and performance measurement.

An up-or-out culture generates high levels of ambition among professionals and selects only the best for further career development. There is only room for the very best on still higher levels in the organization. On the other hand, sticking rigidly to this policy might mean losing many perfectly good employees whose skills are very valuable, even if they have no wish to continue 'climbing the ladder'. But in some firms this is accepted because their standards are the very highest and they have a reputation in the market for being the best professionally and for consistently delivering optimal service. If the firm can stick to its guns, this approach can result in a very efficient business model.

Firms applying the up-or-out principle in the right way have an opportunity to generate a loyal group of former employees as they exit the firm. They may even come to serve as potential new clients in their new jobs, if they are assisted in a constructive way, ensuring that they accept the rationale for the termination of their employment. Provided the professional entered the firm will their eyes wide open, this should be relatively straightforward. In this case, they will have been aware of the firm's strict up-or-out culture, and the steep learning curve, on joining the firm.

Up-and-out cultures go awry only typically when the firm fails to be consistent in following through, or when it fails to soften the transition out of the firm if the professional has not reached the required performance level.

To work effectively, an up-or-out-culture demands several things:

- The continual recruitment of new young professionals substituting those leaving. The recruitment base must function well at all times.
- There should be openings at all levels of the career ladder. Either professionals must continually leave the firm, including professionals at the highest levels, or the firm must be on a sufficient growth path which continually allows for an expansion of the number of employees at the highest levels. As most knowledge-intensive firms have a leverage between senior and junior professionals above 1 (more than one junior for each senior), considerable growth will be needed at the lowest levels to create growth at the highest levels as well.
- There must be a strong professional and personal development for everyone while in the firm. Professionals should receive assistance in obtaining acceptable jobs outside the firm, and a strong alumni policy should be in place to retain loyalty among professionals leaving.

McKinsey & Company operates just such a policy. Many consultants move on to management positions in client companies and a high percentage subsequently return as clients. McKinsey & Company also stages regular alumni events and other activities to consolidate loyalty in various ways.

Ultimately, however, an up-or-out culture is a difficult one to implement consistently, and there are many examples of successful knowledge-intensive firms founded on less rigid progression strategies.

Knowledge sharing

While the caliber of its professionals is one of the greatest assets boasted by a knowledge-intensive firm, skills and experience alone do not make up the total picture. Accumulated industry and skills knowledge is one thing, but efficient, effective operational practice demands client knowledge – built from information that may have been gathered by different people over time. Sharing this knowledge among team members is essential to serving the best interests of the client, and therefore the firm.

Over recent years, knowledge sharing has been a priority in knowledge-intensive firms to enhance high-quality services through the application of all competences present in the firm to any given assignment. Modern technology makes it easier than ever to capture and share very sophisticated information easily and flexibly within and between teams, regardless of how geographically dispersed the members are.

If the essence of the firm is its combined knowledge, a logical consequence is that knowledge sharing will be crucial to that firm's success. While the firm's long-term development should focus on building its competitive position, at an operational level success will depend on the firm's ability to capitalize on existing knowledge. It is hence important that a firm has a structured approach to the ways in which knowledge can be found and applied if constituting value added to an assignment. In such processes co-operation, knowledge sharing, and competence synergy are important parameters.

It is of paramount importance, competitively, to be one step ahead of clients. While they may know their own organization inside out, what they may lack is an impartial holistic view of their business challenges (the wood, rather than the trees), as well as a picture of their market standing in a broader competitive context. Building up this broader picture, which the client itself lacks, is the knowledge-intensive firm's best chance to shine.

The knowledge-intensive firm may specialize in providing expertise in benchmarking to the industry, in applying specific models to analyze progress, or techniques to ensure success, facilitating and inspiring new thoughts and approaches, and so on.

Previous experience gained from a range of similar assignments thus positions the knowledge-intensive firm on a higher level than the client, as long as the professionals in the knowledge-intensive firm are capable of interrogating and harnessing the knowledge obtained across previous assignments.

So how can professionals be motivated to collect and share this valuable information? Knowledge-intensive firms can support knowledge-sharing via a number of incentives that may take the form of one of the following characteristics (Figure 5.2):

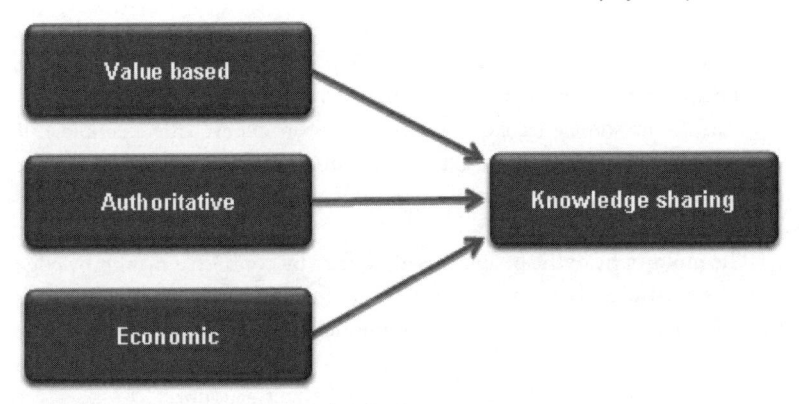

FIGURE 5.2 Incentives for knowledge sharing

- **Value based**: 'this is how we do things in this organization'. This provides a cultural incentive, but also one that appeals to the individual: 'When I help a colleague today, he or she – or another colleague – will help me tomorrow'.
- **Authoritative**: here, sanctions are associated with a lack of adherence to principles, whether related to remuneration, allocation of assignments, or, as a last resort, dismissal.
- **Financial**: reward may be offered for knowledge-sharing, through salary development, bonus, career development, or other benefits complementary to an economic consideration.

As indicated, with today's means of communication, the opportunity for co-operation and knowledge-sharing has improved considerably. Mobile phones, PDAs with integrated telephone and email, intranets and sophisticated remote collaboration environments, and the proliferation of wireless access have accelerated efficiency among professionals.

Consultancies can apply two formal approaches to knowledge management: either a codified (i.e. *systemic* access) or *people-based* access to knowledge. The systemic strategy documents all competences in an IT-supported knowledge management system. Competences acquired in client projects and in other ways are updated and maintained. Colleagues can search for relevant competences to be applied during the sales process and during projects. Ernst & Young was one of the earliest players to adopt a knowledge-sharing system, which it based on the Lotus Notes collaborative environment.

The strength of the systemic strategy is that a systematic overview of competences is present. The weakness is that it takes an enormous amount of updating and a shared understanding of competence levels (what does it mean to be 'somewhat experienced' or a 'top expert', for example?). If the system is not applied or applied inappropriately, the result is a large system demanding a lot of employees' time, yet weakens the organization's knowledge-sharing capability.

The philosophy of the people-based strategy, by contrast, is that knowledge is best shared directly between people. The people-based model emphasizes the collegial relationship and the commitment to the firm and colleagues. Here, competences, approaches, and methods are discussed openly between the knowledge-owners and newcomers to a client account.

The challenge here is to create opportunities and structures that ease the direct communication between professionals in a firm. This could take the form of experience groups, communities of practice (CoPs), and centers of excellence, where people meet and share experiences. Other initiatives might include establishing small café environments, where people can meet over coffee and share knowledge. The strength of the people-based approach is the connection between knowledge and the professional in direct face-to-face communication: the professional is able to convey much more than can be achieved by a short text that has been entered into a computer system. The downside of the people-based approach poses a risk when people change jobs – i.e. that they take their valuable yet undocumented knowledge with them. Even if they have simply moved position within the same firm, the collective memory may be lost if nobody knows where to find it. Further, the right people possessing the right expertise is not always approached, meaning that the firm does not always apply all potentially relevant knowledge to deliver the highest quality.

The effective application of the people-based model demands that management has considerable dedication and that there is some kind of overview – with the result that everyone knows they can contact practice leaders and get assistance – either through direct information or referral to relevant colleagues. The two approaches to knowledge sharing can be illustrated by the model in Table 5.1.

KPMG invests heavily in gathering data on existing and potential clients, but finds that the most valuable information comes from simply spending time on site: 'You read their accounts; you can look at brokers' reports. You can get yourself adequately briefed. But the most important thing is to get out there, to sit down, face to face, and talk', according to a top executive at KPMG.

TABLE 5.1 Strategies for knowledge sharing

	Codification strategy	*Personification strategy*
Structure	Structure of the storage of knowledge	Structure of the communication of co-workers
Personal dimension	Person to document strategy	Person to person strategy
Knowledge sharing	Depersonalized, extract of knowledge	Sharing of knowledge, learning
Higher efficiency	'Economics of reuse'	'Expert economics'
Databases	Key knowledge	Key people
Knowledge arena	The written language	The spoken language

Real curiosity and a desire to make things better are qualities that can't be manufactured, and this enthusiasm will come across to clients:

> If you go out there looking a bit tired, they pick up on it very quickly. Crucially, informal conversations yield information impossible to obtain elsewhere: which competitors a client is working with; how people are remunerated and how this will drive their behavior. Being based at a client's site also means that information can be – and can be seen to be – acted on more quickly. Partners try to spend as much time as they can at clients' sites. Even if they're not working on that particular client, just being there means a client is much more likely to come and talk about things. You can pop into their offices and say, 'I haven't spoken to you for a while and I wondered how things were going'. Clients really value that: even if they've got nothing to tell you, it's given them an opportunity to speak to you' – top executive at KPMG.

This might look effortless to a client, but KPMG's ability to do this isn't accidental: 'You've got to sit and think, whom haven't I met recently? And find reasons to see them.' Moreover, the quid pro quo of getting information is to give it back – both to clients and employees: 'Clients prefer it when information goes both ways. It makes people feel more comfortable.'

Like information gathering, internal communication is more effective when it's informal:

> Formal knowledge-sharing is a lot better than it used to be, but by far the strongest communication channel continues to be our informal

networks – just calling up, finding out what's going on. For all our big jobs, we've taken to doing dinners, rather than formal debriefs, sitting around a room, getting people to talk the good and bad points, but otherwise I don't think we're terribly good at this – we could do more.

In reality, few firms follow either strategy exclusively or to the letter. Many favor applying a degree of technology to facilitate knowledge transfer and knowledge sharing, while relationships play a significant part, too.

Anders Lavesen, of Kromann Reumert, says his organization draws on both approaches. Specifically, it has established an employee-led culture guided by company values; these in turn are supported by concepts and core competence services which are sold successfully in a high-end market:

> However, most important is the culture of knowledge sharing – of finding people with relevant competences, finding documents, standard documents, etc. We have knowledge ambassadors who have specialized knowledge in various areas. Some departments had difficulties convincing themselves that they should upload documents in the shared system. The discussion was: 'What is a specialty, where should it be stored, etc?' There was also an element of nervousness: 'When I upload good documents, will they then be used by others, who are not specialists? Might it hamper my specialization?' But as the years have passed, everyone has realized that it is a good idea. The primary problem is one of priorities: spending time on knowledge sharing. At the moment we have abandoned the idea of a competence database. It is too complicated.
>
> We must be careful about setting up frameworks for the development of professionals, and we should not control everything. On the other hand, we should not give a free rein to the extent that we all wander off in our own direction. Shared guidelines are not a limitation, but a support. Some competitors characterize us as a machine. However, the guidelines support the routines questions so employees can focus their energy on addressing more complex issues. Some applying for a job-seeking experience and then afterwards enter into a commercial career in the business world. Alternatively, people from smaller offices apply. They come to us because they have had enough of anarchy and seek inspiration in our organization.

Research shows that knowledge-intensive firms can be successful by applying both approaches. Either way, it is important that the firm makes a plan and chooses an approach – and is conscious of the implications of that model so that they can play to its strengths without succumbing to its potential weaknesses. It is the management's job to plan and get this right.

Seeing this strategy through must then include measures to ensure employees buy in to the system, and proactively use it to pool and develop their own knowledge (Table 5.2).

Managing stress

Professionals in knowledge-intensive firms tend to work long hours. They are also subject to stress, not only from working hard but potentially arising also from the unclear framework conditions of the job – for instance, lack

TABLE 5.2 Models of knowledge sharing

Channel	Accessibility	Example
Knowledge storage	Accessibility of knowledge	Intranet Databases Folders
Knowledge dispersal	Proliferation	Mail News pages Personnel magazines
Knowledge exposure	Visibility	Wall pictures Noticeboards Visible testimony about the firm's production
Knowledge transfer	Reception	Classroom teaching E-learning Talks and presentations
Knowledge sharing	Communicability	Videoconferences Telephone Chat Mail
Collectivization of knowledge	Cohesion	Mentor programs 'Communities of practice' Informal talk Meetings

Source: Jacoby Petersen and Poulfelt (2002).

of clear goals, poor resource allocation, lack of commitment, and so on. All of which call for good management if they are to be alleviated.

Fifteen years ago, professionals did not have mobile phones, mobile email, or access to a company intranet from home, so it was easier to draw a line between work and home life. Now, endlessly blinking BlackBerrys and access-anywhere company systems intrude on professionals' personal lives to a degree when many find it hard to ignore calls and emails when 'off duty'. This doesn't do any favors to the individual or the firm. A burnt-out, stressed exhausted employee is no good to anyone, and may need more time off in the long term if a stress-related illness takes hold.

The professional labor market has been radically transformed over the last decade or more, and this can be seen in other ways too. Individuals can be involved in many projects at a time, working on the one while traveling to another. Virtual teams can be formed with colleagues in other countries too, thanks to sophisticated collaboration and communications facilities.

On the plus side, today's technology can also be used to take *back* some control, enabling professionals to work more flexibly from home, eliminating the commute, and enabling them to fit in more readily with family life. Ubiquitous connectivity can also reduce stress by enabling continuity of contact when stuck in traffic, delayed at an airport, or where meetings are running late.

Modern technology presents the ability to find more efficient solutions for clients, enabling the delivery of higher quality through greater access to relevant information and pooled knowledge. The challenge is finding a way to make technology work for the company and its professionals, and not against them. If technology increases rather than alleviates professional stress, this is not a positive development.

Bo Netterstrøm is a leading Scandinavian specialist in occupational health and stress. He notes that stress is often characterized by a feeling that a person is not in control of their job situation and important decisions. High levels of control and overview might thus facilitate a balanced working life, while low levels of control might trigger stress (see Table 5.3).

Stress occurs relatively frequently in knowledge-intensive firms due to the associated high levels of work pressure. With reference to Netterstrøm's research, it is important however to establish that short-term stress (for example, in connection with deadline-related strain) is not particularly negative in the sense that it leads to disease. In other words, stress only becomes a problem after a long period of high tension (Figure 5.3).

Other, more damaging stress should be avoided through strong management, where possible. A lack of balance between the demands of an assignment and the competence levels of the professional may elicit

TABLE 5.3 Netterstrøm's demand-control model

	High level of control	Low level of control
High demands	Activity	Strain
Low demands	Relaxation	Passivity

Reproduced with permission from Bo Netterstrøm. Stress på arbejdspladsen.
© Gyldendal Academic Group, 2002.

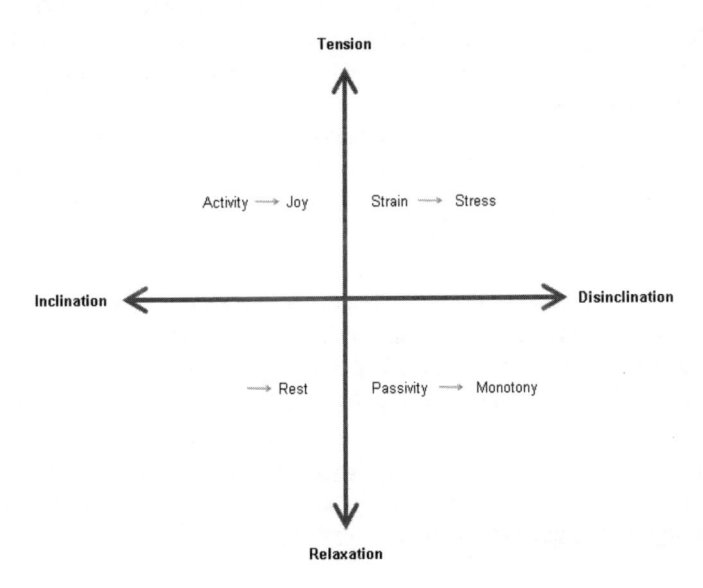

FIGURE 5.3 Netterstrøm's illustration of the connection between the demand-control model and stress
Source: Reproduced with permission from Bo Netterstrøm. Stress på arbejdspladsen.
© Gyldendal Academic Group, 2002.

considerable stress in some workers – particularly if managers are not aware of this and do not provide support and training.

A management consultant told one of the authors:

> If I feel I am in control of my assignments and what I deliver, I am able to work 70 hours a week for several weeks without feeling pressure or stress. If I do not quite feel I am in charge of my assignments, I may feel stressed even if I work only 37 hours a week.

Task assignment is an important factor not only in the development of an individual professional but also in terms of their wellbeing and 'happiness' at work. It is one thing for an employee to be stretched but another to feel out of their depth, vulnerable, and in danger of doing a bad job.

Managers should therefore attempt to find a coherent balance between professionals' desire for development and their ability to handle a given task. They should also provide access to the appropriate tools and resources available to enable them to handle and control the assignment.

Another stress creator among some professionals is a lack of balance between the professional's expectations and ambitions, and the extent to which their efforts are recognized and appreciated by the organization. This emphasizes the need for sustained honest, concrete, and direct feedback in annual performance reviews.

Culturally, the management must establish a level of ambition concerning what is expected of professionals. Again, this should be with a clear focus on the individual: just because a father of young children has a preference for working less, other colleagues – who may or may not have children – should not be deterred from working more if they can or want to. A flexible culture also demands that colleagues accept each other's preferences, ambitions, and positions in working and family life.

Help cannot be offered unless problems are spotted, however, so managers need to be vigilant about looking out for any signs of strain among professionals. If they identify stress-related behavior, be it employees who find it difficult to say no or in other ways seem strained, it is the duty of the manager to take immediate action and prioritize assignments in order to ensure a reasonable workload.

Summary

This chapter has examined the complex needs of professionals as they join and move through a knowledge-intensive firm, and the ways that managers can maximize their performance, development, and wellbeing during their time with the company.

Having noted the central importance of professionals in creating and delivering the value presented to clients, we have emphasized the need to be selective in the skill and experience profiles targeted during recruitment drives and have emphasized that professionals constitute the capital in knowledge-intensive firms.

As we have noted, although there is a fine line between over- and under-managing talent, leaders need to be vigilant and proactive at all times, in making sure star performers remain challenged, middle-ground players are not neglected, and that there is a solid strategy for bringing low achievers on – or for moving them on.

Professionals demand the presence of management at certain times to develop by feedback and coaching and the absence of management at other times to develop by independence and responsibility. The application of these two management styles must be adjusted individually to each professional.

Questions for reflection

- Are professionals central to your firm's creation of value? To what extent is the quality provided created by the professionals?
- If professionals are the capital in your firm, how does the firm manage this capital with a view to optimizing the firm's profits?
- Does the firm regularly measure the satisfaction and development of professionals?
- Where is your firm positioned on a scale from 1 to 10 (where 1 is inferior and 10 superior) in terms of management performance, when it comes to responding to the high- or low-touch needs of individuals?

6

SHAPING BEHAVIOR: VALUES AND CULTURAL MODELING

Having considered the complexities of managing talented individuals, it is now important to consider the interplay between the needs of the organization and the needs of professionals, and how knowledge-intensive firms can balance the two to create win–win scenarios.

Having noted already that, in the context of knowledge-intensive firms, independent professionals will often be working fairly autonomously on client assignments, we explore the importance of value-based management as a means of ensuring that their actions and approaches align with the firm's explicit strategy and agreed priorities (Figure 6.1).

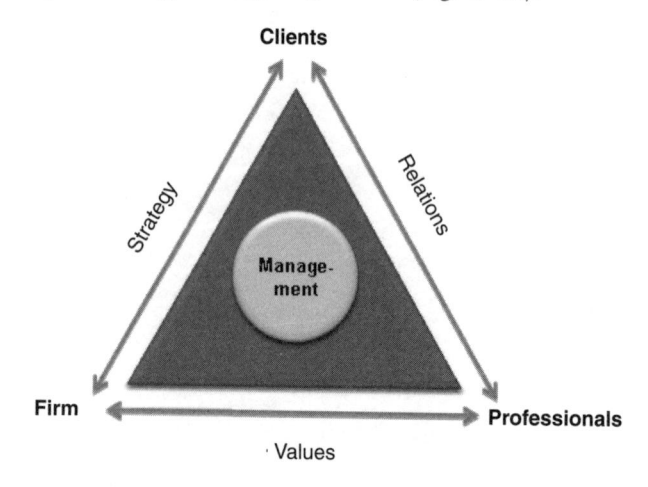

FIGURE 6.1 Value-driven knowledge-intensive firms

Strategic action

For the knowledge-intensive firm, the development of strategy is not just about identifying the most lucrative markets and a strong business model to address them. It also relies on creating cohesion between the strategy and the firm's professionals. Professionals must buy into the strategy and the choices that will need to be made to ensure this is executed properly – for example, the types of work they agree to, how teams will be leveraged, and so on.

Typically, knowledge-intensive firms have a minimal hierarchy, favoring considerable delegation of responsibility to professionals, in terms of delivering assignments and sales. By definition, then, strategies in knowledge-intensive firms are implemented by professionals – in their decisions, behavior, and actions. This is expressed in the way they work and the way they apply methodologies; in the relationship they establish with the client and the way interaction is managed; and in the prioritization of time on a given task. This applies in both the public and private sectors.

To ensure everyone aligns there will need to be a clearly set out strategy, with defined and agreed goals and values. Without these, there can be no hope of consistency. Once they are in place, however, professionals will be able to prioritize more easily and make informed decisions in assignments and sales. We refer to this as the 'strategic action' of the firm.

Managers are unlikely to have complete knowledge of what goes on in their organization and on all client assignments in detail. Nor will they have the capacity to make all the required choices, or to act as a guiding factor in all decisions that are made. This is as it should be: it would detract from the needs of professionals for responsibility and independence. Managers seeking to control all decision-making will create problems for the organization in terms of its ability to retain competent employees with the ability to think independently.

This does not mean fully relinquishing control, however. Managers of knowledge-intensive firms should instead be prepared to navigate a role of negotiation and persuasion. They must lead by example and champion the behavior required of professionals. We refer to this as an organization's 'cultural modeling'. This requires a management discipline based on values – values that have been defined by managers, and which are used to influence the behavior and choices of the professionals in their daily actions on tasks and in sales.

In the public sector, the UK Department for Work and Pensions has put considerable care and thought into defining four core values, which steer its professionals' work. These are set out on its website:

- Achieving the best – using all our resources efficiently so that high and consistent standards of service are provided.
- Respecting people – treating our clients and each other with respect, welcoming diversity and valuing others' ideas and responding fairly to individual needs.
- Making a difference – supporting, challenging and inspiring clients to improve their lives and helping each other to make a difference
- Looking outwards – working with others and learning how to get better at what we do. (http://www.dwp.gov.uk/about-dwp/vision-aims-and-values/)

Within this overall context, the department has developed a competency framework, outlining how people are expected to deliver the objectives and 'live' the values – something that requires a lot of care and effort, as Director of Corporate HR and HR Strategy, Jaqui Perryer, explains:

> Our values are particularly important because, in common with other government organizations in the aftermath of the recession, we're entering a period of unprecedented change and uncertainty. We are such a complex organization that having a single mission statement is not easy. But we're also very operationally focussed, so we tend to be fact-based and target-driven rather than inspired by values.
>
> When people here read or listen to messages from the most senior people in the department, they won't always hear their voice or the values that are implied. Values need to be more than words on a page. Employees have to see that senior managers live the values, but one of our challenges here is the sheer scale of our organization and the distance this creates between the top and bottom of the hierarchy. To counteract this, one of the initiatives we run is a 'back to the floor program' in which senior civil servants spend time working on the frontline alongside our client-facing staff. It's a way of demonstrating that the values apply at all levels, as well as a means of connecting these senior people with the challenges facing front-line staff.

Høier, at UMKC, the *visibility* of an organization's values – and of their application by managers – is critical to ensuring they are applied consistently by professionals across the board:

> There is a pressure for visible management. It is not sufficient that I, the manager, formulate clear visible goals for my employees. It is just

as important that I spend time with my employees, demonstrating that I am serious about this – that it is not just something I write on a piece of paper. This signifies two things: 1) it is not what you say, it is what you do that's important; and 2) that visible management also entails that sometimes the employees do not accept what I say. Sometimes I have made decisions, but they do not accept them, perhaps because it clips their wings.

This highlights another challenge facing managers as they attempt to guide and influence the behavior of their professionals – that of not demotivating them in the process. But, again, value-based management can help here.

Says Høier:

> There is a trend in the labour market where employees' demands for self-development on the job is intensified. The products we deliver become increasingly knowledge-intensive - also in production companies and service companies. This creates a demand for autonomous thought processes in the workforce. The employees must be able to take independent action, and innovate. These days, changes happen with considerable speed, so it becomes increasingly difficult to construct heavy bureaucratic systems that can handle everything. You have to create some guidelines and a value-based management in order to persuade people to take the options you recommend.

Trusting them to follow agreed behavior is one way of keeping professionals motivated so that they work in a way that meets the needs and priorities of the firm. This sense of fulfillment can then be further supplemented by other strategies for making professionals feel appreciated and fulfilled. Being in the public sector, the UMKC has to think beyond salary packages, so it favors a staff-development strategy based on skills development and training:

> In the public sector, we are not at the vanguard of salary development. Hence it is even more important that we are able to offer people a job with potential for development and work activities that people feel are worthwhile. Today employees have enormous demands in terms of self-realization, particularly at work, so it is important that they are able to identify with work that it is meaningful – Høier at UMKC.

This means giving them an influence – or at least a feeling of influence – over the work they do, even if there need to be some agreed parameters on how they approach this.

As intelligent repositories of significant knowledge in their field, professionals do not like to be confronted with a *fait accompli*. They want to be involved – in decisions about their career development, the work they do, and how they do it – and to feel that they are heard and worth consulting. They want influence. Decisions must be discussed before set in stone. Even if they don't agree with the final outcome, they will appreciate having had a chance to contribute to the discussion.

Clearly it helps enormously if the professional's values, needs, and goals mirror those of the company they work for. Professionals who don't agree with the firm's goals will soon become dissatisfied.

It is also important that the firm's mission statements reflect the actual goals of the firm, as envisioned by the management. If the cited goals aren't borne out in everyday decision-making and actions, this will soon become evident to professionals who will feel compromised. If management does not mean or do what it says, it will only get away with this for so long – and not in critical situations where importance choices must be made.

When discussing strategy involving employees, the following questions might be useful as a basis for discussion, to ensure that everyone understands the common purpose:

Clients

- What type of clients do we want?
- What do our clients feel we do best?
- Who are our key clients?
- What sales strategy should we apply?

Competitors

- Who are our competitors?
- Which competitors do we want to outmaneuver?
- What would be the worst thing our competitors could do to us?
- What are our strengths and our weaknesses compared with the competitors?

The firm

- What business are we in?

- Who are we?
- What do we find exciting and interesting to do?
- What are we best at?
- Recruitment: what type of professionals should we recruit?
- Strategic competence development: which competences should we teach professionals in order to implement our strategy?
- Promotions and rewards: what behavior and which results should be rewarded?
- What is our pricing policy?
- Are we striving to create growth or profitability?

Resource management

Appropriate resource allocation is another potential bone of contention between professionals and the firm, if strategic priorities have not been aligned effectively. Clearly, a successful delivery will depend heavily on the availability of appropriate skills and in sufficient number when they are needed. At the same time, a professional's ability to do their job properly, and to be seen to be doing it properly, will be compromised if they don't have the support they need when they need it. In addition to disappointing the client, this will reflect badly on the team involved, undermining their sense of job satisfaction and ongoing motivation. Adequate management focus must therefore be applied to resource allocation – i.e. deciding which professionals should work on which assignments and in which team configurations.

There are two business-critical reasons why this is important:

1. To a significant extent, the professional's competence development happens during assignments. Professionals are very aware of this fact and so will attempt to influence allocation decisions. Managers need to be sensitive to this fact and attempt to strike the right balance between the needs of the professional and the needs of the business and its clients.
2. An optimal application of resources is a profit driver in the knowledge-intensive firm – field too many heavy-weight professionals and the cost of servicing the client will soar, with implications either for the fees the firm must charge or for the hit it will take to the profitability of the engagement.

The challenge, then, is to allocate resources in a way that ensures the best use of the firm's cumulative employee resources, while tallying with the firm's business model. Ensuring short and long-term success – in terms of quality, development of competences in the firm, as well as with the individual professional, retention, and profits – will depend on carefully combining these resources.

Assignment allocation

As we have seen already, ambitious professionals naturally strive for constant challenges and continual development through new assignments which require that they push themselves to their limits. This means that they are likely to have strong preferences about the projects to which they are assigned. Allocating individuals to the right assignments is of vital importance to their development and self-esteem. The most exciting, interesting, and demanding tasks with high learning and development potential are deemed to be the most prestigious. It follows, then, that professionals who are 'chosen' for particularly complex tasks will feel special – that they have somehow been singled out for preferential treatment. Those passed over, meanwhile, may feel that they are somehow less well thought of or not deemed up to the challenge. In this way, the allocation of assignments can indicate a hierarchy in knowledge-intensive firms, even if this does not exist overtly.

In other scenarios, it may simply be that individuals have developed a preference for certain tasks, and are perhaps trying to carve out a niche for themselves. They may become frustrated if they do not get a chance to work with precisely the area that interests them the most. This can create tension in an organization.

If this happens, and someone is developing a prima-donna attitude to their preferred work, action may need to be taken. While it is important to oblige the needs of the professionals where possible, it is also important to motivate them to understand that there are other assignments to complete as well and that, if everyone cherry-picked the best jobs, no one would do the bread-and-butter work which also pays their salary. Inspiring professionals to focus on the exciting aspects of all tasks, and to appreciate the need for an element of fairness, may be difficult but is important.

Lotte Grünbaum, former Manager of Center for Corporate Administration CFK in the Danish Ministry of the Environment, describes the challenge:

> People are not pleased if they are not allowed to work with something that interests them, and if they are not happy, the quality of the solution might suffer. Hence, one should motivate them to be happy and content. The major challenge is to get as many people as possible to do what they are pleased to do and good at.

The Danish communication firm, Masters, has invested a lot of effort into achieving this and prides itself on its ability to deliver a fulfilling work experience to its employees. The firm's vision is set out on its website as follows:

> In terms of communication, we create value in co-operation with motivated people!
>
> We know what we want. Our lives are too short to associate with people who are not motivated. It is our right and our duty to say no thank you, when we experience a lack of will. We want to investigate the cause of the lack of interest. We want to understand – and then move on together happily – or go our separate ways.
>
> In terms of communication, we want to make a visible difference. We believe that intelligent communication is THE single most important factor in the business strategies of the future. We want to create value that benefits the sender, the receiver, and ourselves. (www.masters.dk)

Fortunately, professionals will vary in their priorities and preferences for different types of assignments, allowing a natural division of work. Depending on the individual, the prized element of each task may be the client itself, the task to be performed, the industry coverage or geographical outreach, or the configuration of the team. Where a manager is unable to accommodate everyone's preferences, solid criteria will be needed to establish a fair distribution of assignments over time.

Ultimately, however, there will be battles over the best projects, and the hard fact of the matter is that the firm will want to field its best people if there is a lot at stake – for example, the long-term business of an important new client. As a result, those with the best professional skills are likely to have their preferences fulfilled more often than others. Keeping the peace and ensuring that other staff are 'brought on', however, means that the needs of other team players are considered on a case-by-case basis.

The battle for the best projects will be familiar to knowledge-intensive firms across all sectors. Lotte Grümbaum explains the dilemma from the professional's perspective:

> People are busy, but then that big project comes along that can boost your career. Because it's important, your boss has a better chance of seeing what you're doing. So people fight to get onto the project, even though they are very busy already. Then it's a case of who should

be allocated to that project and be given the opportunity? Should you go for the elite, the talented, or look more broadly? You tend to give it to the elite, because as a manager you also want that important assignment completed in the best possible way.

Elizabeth Maddison, at the Institute of Development Studies, agrees that this issue is present in the public sector:

> Our projects vary widely in their scope and scale. They can occupy several people for much of their time for three to five years or a single researcher some of the time for a few months. But which projects we bid for and who works on them tends to be decided by the academic Fellows, individually or in small groups – it's all highly autonomous and quite fluid. They may see something that plays to their expertise and interests, or they may spend time working with funders to develop and articulate new areas for investigation. The process is almost wholly self-managed.

That is, however, changing:

> There are already more projects which involve us working in consortia with other academic and private sector institutions both in the UK and globally, and these require more planning and a much greater investment of time to prepare a proposal and program support to deliver it successfully. Increasingly, we respond to funding opportunities that require particular types of partnership and a mix of 'inputs' and, increasingly, we deliver programs with a mix of staff, Fellows working alongside communications experts for example, and with colleagues who are based in the global south. One of the interesting issues is that Fellows differ in how well they do in reaching the 180 days' funding target. Some regularly exceed that, some find it much more difficult, and we know that new Fellows at the start of their IDS career tend to find it more challenging. The current system means too that we're not particularly strategic about areas that we may want to subsidize because we know they won't easily cover their costs but we regard them as highly valuable. There may be lots of good reasons why some areas – and Fellows – find funding more difficult than others, and fashion amongst funders will be one. So far we're managed that by keeping the overall balance positive and by supporting individuals to be flexible. But in an increasingly difficult funding climate – greater

competition for funds, much greater scrutiny of value for money, and pressure on margins – we probably need to do more and more actively to balance the 'supply side' and 'demand side' aspects to our work. I think there is an underlying trend here of starting to see the overall research program as a more managed portfolio; alongside even greater efforts at senior levels in the institute to get close to funders and really understand their priorities.

Encouraging professionals to cope with more variety and assume tasks outside their comfort zone is important too, not only out of fairness but so that the great don't get greater at the expense of the career development of less experienced staff. To keep everyone fresh, challenged, and satisfied, a degree of rotation will be required.

Success here demands that managers know the preferences and needs of each individual. In conclusion, the allocation of resources to assignments is balancing the demands of professionals toward competence development and company profits. Specialists should be doing the same assignment over and over to extend profitability. On the other hand, specialists may prefer to develop new skills instead of doing the same over and over. The dilemma should be solved by ensuring that the specialist will do some routine assignments while also having new challenges.

Client selection

Once these needs and preferences are known, the knowledge-intensive firm can use this information as one of its guiding principles when selecting which business to bid for. Anders Lavesen takes the following approach to client selection:

> Specialization means a lot to us, but we are also full-service. We are not only there for the large companies; we are also experts in servicing medium-size firms – an important market for us to develop for the benefit for our professionals and partners. Often the problems being experienced by our clients are the same whether they are large or small. By working with smaller clients, we gain experience that we can apply in the larger cases. If we concentrated on large cases exclusively, we would not be as big as we are – or so specialized – because Denmark is such a small country. We have to retain the medium-sized companies in order to get the volume to achieve the necessary specialization.

In addition, it is attractive and prestigious for younger people to work for medium-sized companies. In large cases, juniors are often far from the front line. In smaller cases, they have a chance to get much closer because the team is smaller. Smaller cases also teach us how to handle client relations.

Weighing up potential assignments in the light of the value they will create for the supplier organization and its professionals is important, from both a short and long-term perspective.

If any lack of profitability is compensated for by the learning potential or prospects for future business, there may be value in pursuing the work. If, however, there is any danger the engagement will backfire in some way – perhaps because resources are lacking, the assignment falls outside the normal remit, or the project will not be profitable given the budget and other constraints – it may be better, strategically, to leave it alone.

Here are some considerations to take into account when calculating the opportunity for value creation from a potential assignment:

Short term

- Does the firm possess the necessary resources and competences to deliver effectively?
- Will the assignment or the client contribute to an efficient application of resources?
- Does the assignment fit into the market in which the firm operates?

Long term

- Will the assignment or the client contribute to the efficient accumulation of resources and competences related to the firm's strategy?
- Will the assignment or the client strengthen or weaken the firm's control of the accumulated resources and competences? (While challenging assignments can help in the retention of good professionals who appreciate the training potential of the tasks, assignments that are perceived as dull by good workers could undermine their loyalty to the firm and trigger employee mobility.)

As we have discussed in previous chapters, it will also be important to consider the extent to which any new offer of work fits within the agreed firm and market strategy. In order to generate value, the strategy must be borne out by the selected business model and be executed in daily decisions and behavior by management and professionals. Likewise, recruitment, professionals' development, and the company's sales strategy must be planned in accordance with the strategy.

Danish communication firm, Masters, looks for 'experience' and 'will' in the people it hires, because these are the qualities which will best enable team members to deliver, according to founder Søren Schnedler:

> First and foremost, we look for the ability and the will to co-operate. [New employees] must have a substantial commitment to making a difference if they are to contribute to the creation of value and chemistry. We are a people business, so we also have an excess of relatively experienced people.

UK consulting firm Xantus is another knowledge-intensive firm which pays close attention to its recruitment strategy to ensure it fits with the firm's broader strategy. Says Chief Executive Steve Watmough:

> Like every consulting firm, we have to keep evolving, moving out into new markets and developing new services – and that means that the profile of people we recruit has changed over time. We still need and still recruit deep technical specialists in specific areas. However, as we've taken on broader roles and more strategic projects, we've required other skills to complement these technical ones. We'd compare it to the difference between a builder and an architect. If you want to extend your house, you're going to needed a builder to do the actual construction work, but you also need an architect. The architect's role is to work with the client to take their ideas and translate them into a plan which the builder can follow, and to ensure that the extension is built to the design. As we grow and take on bigger, more high-profile projects, it's these 'architectural' skills we'll need more of.

Watmough is also acutely aware that Xantus needs people who are prepared to work in a specific way:

> One of the things we hear repeatedly from clients is that we're different to the big consulting firms. We don't rush to bring in large teams of consultants, but prefer to put a small team in who can work alongside our clients just like their own employees. Rather than trying

to sell the next piece of work, we have people who are genuinely committed to seeing the project they're working on through to its successful conclusion. This means that clients see the 'whole' person: we don't recruit one-sided people who just do their job and leave.

Cultural modeling

The firms interviewed for this book present a strong case in favor of cultural modeling being important to ensure execution of strategy and, hence, long-term success. Cultural modeling is not a simple management task. It is about instilling a fundamental set of values into the organization (i.e. the professionals) in their daily operations and decisions.

The firms we approached during our research signaled a shared focus on the creation of a strong culture with room for individual realization of ambitions – in a team-driven organization. Various ownership structures, meanwhile, suggest that there is a broad spectrum of conditions in which the creation of such a culture can be achieved.

Rambøll, the largest Scandinavian engineering consultancy of 10,000 employees, is a 60-year-old firm which has evolved over the years according to the philosophy of founder Børge Rambøll. In particular, this has meant the business following a path of corporate social responsibility (CSR) decades before the business world started to talk about this as a discrete discipline. At Rambøll, CSR is expressed via a strong value-based firm which focusses on the development of employees and societal responsibility. This is also reflected in the ownership structure. Rambøll and two other founders established a foundation which majority owns the company (there is also approximately 5 percent employee ownership, giving professionals a solid feeling of 'buy in' to the business).

Flemming Bligaard Pedersen, Rambøll's CEO, has this to say about the balance between professionals' desire for development and the company's strategic course:

> Personal development is the employees' first, second, and third priority. Managers must consolidate the strategy they agree on, but also motivate the professionals. Hence you cannot purge a company and streamline everybody. We must attempt to do some development, otherwise I cannot hold on to them. We must see it as a developmental process.

> Rambøll's homepage expands on the company's philosophy:
>
> It is Rambøll's vision that employees should thrive in an open, trusting and multi-cultural working environment characterized by cohesion, decentralized management, extended competence delegation and personal development.
>
> As a knowledge-intensive firm, employees' competences and enthusiasm are Rambøll's most important resource. We focus on offering our employees good conditions for competence development.
>
> Development on personal and professional levels increases the employees' value at Rambøll, while also increasing their value in the labor market. At Rambøll, competence development entails training in both professional and personal skills. (www.ramboll.dk)

Flemming Bligaard Pedersen considers professionals as 'people with knowledge' who build their own careers concurrently with the development of the company. Inevitably, this poses some management challenges – for example, professionals need to feel they are doing meaningful work while establishing a team culture during projects:

> It is an individualist culture. If you are not careful, professionals might each develop in their own direction. Being people with knowledge, they are well educated and have their own opinions. This means they behave as lone wolves. Where possible, they need to be given a shared framework, a shared platform, so that they can be themselves, but within agreed parameters. They must feel they have a role to play, in their own way, otherwise they will leave. But all projects require a team culture.

UK-based engineering firm, Arup, is another firm keen to motivate its employees by giving them maximum involvement and ownership of their work. The business ownership, like Rambøll, takes the form of a trust, managed for the benefit of employees and their dependents. With no shareholders or external investors, the firm is able to determine its own direction as a business and set its own priorities. Each of Arup's employees receives a share of the firm's operating profit each year. Says partner Volker Buscher:

Not having to return profits to an external party is a huge strength for us. Because we don't have external shareholders, we don't have to return our profits to them and we can choose whether to invest them in our capabilities or share them with our employees. This is also hugely important as we look to develop our environment-related services: the structure we have, and the values it gives us, enable us to take a long view. Our belief in stewardship, our responsibility of managing our firm so that it will be successful to future generations of employees, is mirrored in the services we provide.

Partner-owned knowledge-intensive firms have an advantage in that they are able to ensure close ties between their professionals and the partners of the business they become part of – from whom they learn client service and receive training, and so on. Partner ownership also creates dynamic sales, because the partner 'owns' a client whom they single-handedly develop and cultivate (a key account management approach – see Chapter 7).

The partner structure also establishes a number of smaller operations within the same firm, because the partner often has a relatively independent position in their market, with clients and employees. This means that it can be more difficult to implement uniform management standards, however, because management is culture and culture requires a consistent interpretation of challenges, remedies, and actual execution.

Dealing with deviance

Earlier we noted that professionals need to *see* management dedication in order to believe in an organization's strategy. They must also see evidence of sanctions being imposed where there is systematic non-compliance with strategic priorities. The professionals must agree to standards that have been set down, and to consistent adherence to them – or at least the *ambition* to meet standards every time. Where professionals fall short, there must be consequences to avoid the firm's reputation being eroded and its future growth potential being undermined.

To ensure that people do not get away with not being competent to do their job or unwilling to meet standards, performance should be monitored. Professionals with weaknesses must be encouraged, helped, supported, trained, and coached to gain the necessary skills to enable them to meet standards. If no progress is seen, the company must enforce sanctions, ultimately dismissing the professional if an *impasse* has been reached.

Clearly, this is a last resort. Taking such extreme action after an isolated mistake would suggest a zero-tolerance culture, which many firms would be unable to live with as it would preclude innovation and development. Many knowledge-intensive firms make a living by being innovative, spotting new trends and opportunities, inventing new ways of doing things, and testing new approaches with the clients. Most professionals are attracted by such a culture. A zero-tolerance culture would create a static environment which would erode skills development and, in turn, the firm's ability to deliver value to clients. Worst of all, the best professionals would probably leave.

In situations where a zero-tolerance culture is essential due to the nature of the work – for example, where safety is an issue – recruitment strategies will need to emphasize and be geared toward professionals and managers who are motivated by this type of culture.

A sudden dismissal is never a good idea. Continuous feedback should be in place, enabling early warnings that something is not up to standard so that remedial action can be taken. Without such mechanisms, the chance to nip problems in the bud and turn a problem into a learning opportunity is missed. This, in turn, means that any effort and investment expended on the given professional up to that point has been in vain.

Handle the situation well, on the other hand, and it is an important signal to other employees: there is no need to panic and fear that you will be next in line but, rather, that, if you do not live up to the standards of the organization, you will be told as part of a standard feedback process, giving you a full opportunity to address any problems before further action is taken.

Of course, it is essential that the manager is very conscious of the extent of a problem once it has been identified. If a manager loses confidence in an employee, it may be very difficult to re-establish this, even following new training. A lack of confidence in an employee's abilities often results in a focus on the negative. This makes it difficult for the manager to give praise where it is due, resulting in a downward spiral as the professional's self-belief is further dented, and their enthusiasm sapped.

Once a manager has become aware of a problem, they should be discreet about the situation and sincerely attempt to help and develop the person in question using strategies they have faith in as a means of achieving positive results.

Where all practical solutions have been exhausted, and the professional does not have a future in the firm, the best way forward is to provide positive assistance to help the given member of staff move on as quickly as possible – to a job more suited to their skills, experience, and potential.

Knowledge-intensive firms boast many good examples of employees who have stopped developing in a particular company, who go on to find new jobs in which they thrive and bloom.

Taking decisive action is preferable to keeping an underperforming professional in the firm for too long. This can drain time and resources, while risking a loss of face for the manager among the rest of the staff – having been seen not to have acted effectively. If the knock-on effect is that other professionals have to pick up the slack, working overtime to ensure work is completed (often at short notice), this will do nothing to endear the manager to the rest of the team.

Value-based management

We have already touched on the importance of 'values' as a means by which knowledge-intensive firms can steer and guide their professionals to delivering against company strategy. Values are the structural pivot in many professionally run knowledge-intensive firms, because in this type of firm they can stimulate more independence and self-management than more traditional forms of management control.

McKinsey & Company was probably the first knowledge-intensive firm to begin managing its business on the basis of a set of fixed values. As early as the 1930s, founder Marvin Bower formulated a set of 'beliefs' or rules to live by, which have been followed by the firm ever since. Today many of these original values are still followed, articulated by the firm in the words below, which can be found on McKinsey & Company's website:

> We believe in professionalism. For us, this means to always:

- *Put the client's interest ahead of our own.* This means we deliver more value than expected. It doesn't mean doing whatever the client asks.
- *Behave as professionals.* Uphold absolute integrity. Show respect to local custom and culture, as long as we don't compromise our integrity.
- *Keep our client information confidential.* We don't reveal sensitive information. We don't promote our own good work. We focus on making our clients successful.
- *Tell the truth as we see it.* We stay independent and able to disagree, regardless of the popularity of our views or their effect on our fees. We have the courage to invent and champion unconventional solutions to problems. We do this to help build internal support, get to real issues, and reach practical recommendations.

- *Deliver the best of our firm to every client as cost effectively as we can.* We expect that our people spend clients' and our firm's resources as if their own resources were at stake. (www.mckinsey.com/aboutus/whatwebelieve)

These values are sound rules to live by. They are also easy to relate to and to teach to new professionals and, because they are an integral part of the philosophy behind the performance of assignments and McKinsey & Company's incentive structure, the firm's strategy and execution all adds up.

To get to this point, values must be executed by management so that they can in turn be executed by professionals. Values should support and guide professionals in their everyday work. If they do not, they are just window-dressing: showy, but insignificant. Unfortunately, this is the case for many knowledge-intensive firms – consider the many hypocritical law firms which promise new recruits a value system that 'takes both career and private life into account', when in reality they expect staff to work very long hours and to take case notes home.

Value systems are important management tools in the public sector, too. Ordnance Survey, Britain's national mapping agency, sets out the following value-based aims on its website:

> Creating the definitive geographic database: Our investment in global positioning systems, aerial photography and new surveying techniques enables us to constantly update, enhance and maintain our database with at least 5,000 changes every day. This expertise enables us to provide our clients with an accurate, up-to-date and detailed geographic framework covering the whole country.
>
> Delivering intelligent geographic data: We are delivering the most detailed and sophisticated geographic information resource for any country in the world.
>
> OS Mastermap offers a new national standard in digital mapping, which enables different pieces of information to be linked together and exchanged to help cut costs, enhance services and improve decision making in a common framework.
>
> Collaborating to provide creative information solutions: We are continually developing new ways to deliver geographic information in response to industry trends and market demand to meet the ever-changing needs of our clients. As a recognized industry leader, we also play an active role in standards bodies such as the World Wide Web Consortium and the Open Geospatial Consortium. We are also driving the development of the Digital National Framework (DNF) to create an open standards approach to geographic information use.

Championing innovation and technology: We work with a wide range of organizations to champion excellence in the use of geographic information and maximize client choice. Our approach includes research and innovation projects, joint initiatives in both the public and private sector and an international engagement program to aid the global exchange of ideas, expertise and best practice. We have an extensive network of partners who use their expertise, skills and knowledge to add values to our data by creating applications and solutions for a wide range of business and consumer markets.

Benefiting the nation as a self-funding government department: Independent experts calculate that around 10 percent of Great Britain's economic activity is dependent upon our data. We are financed through data licensing rather than direct funding from the taxpayer and, as a Trading Fund, are responsible for our own finances and business planning. Through projects, such as our Free Maps for 11-year-olds initiative, we are committed to using our expertise and resources to realize social, environmental and economic benefits for our staff, the local community, the nation and beyond. (http://www.ordnancesurvey.co.uk/oswebsite/aboutus/corporatemessages/index html)

Summary

In this chapter we have developed a central premise that, since the strategies of knowledge-intensive firms are implemented in the professionals' daily actions and decisions, value-based management is a valuable tool for consolidating strategic actions – i.e. for ensuring that professionals follow through and deliver on the firm's vision.

Value-based management, in turn, is delivered through continuous cultural modeling, where professionals experience company values through the actions taken by management. Managers' dialog with professionals about company values and their implementation is also an important element.

We have also noted that business strategy and professional strategy must be consistent and support each other. The development of professionals is crucial in knowledge-intensive firms and, given that this occurs to a large degree through live assignments, allocation of assignments is a central developmental process – ideally resulting in employee satisfaction and professional advancement. Similarly, consideration must be given to *resource* allocation, so that the client receives quality solutions delivered at highest efficiency, while professionals are adequately supported in their work. As we have indicated, these issues apply across both the private and public sectors.

Values help establish the guidelines, provide support for the firm's strategy, and help professionals execute company strategy and goals.

Questions for reflection

- Has your firm formulated an explicit set of values which is known to all professionals?
- Do your firm's professionals regularly see you and the rest of the management team executing company values in your own actions?
- Where would you position your firm on a scale from 1 to 10 (where 1 is inferior and 10 superior) in terms of consolidating professionals' development as a central parameter in the allocation of assignments?

7
RELATIONS WITH CLIENTS RULE STRATEGY EXECUTION

In the pyramid model we have set out and which we are exploring throughout this book, another crucial dimension is the interplay between the professionals (who represent the supplier organization) and the client. This is because it is through the interaction between professionals and the client organization that value is created for clients – and thus for the knowledge-intensive firm (Figure 7.1).

This is the focus of the current chapter. Again, the operative dynamics of this situation are best illustrated using real examples.

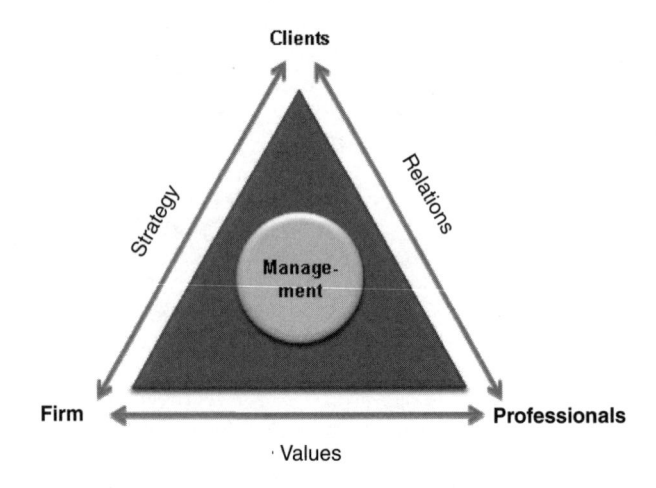

FIGURE 7.1 Relations between clients and professionals in knowledge-intensive firms

Sales based on trust

An obvious place to start examining the dynamics of this relationship is the sales process – the process by which the two parties enter into a relationship. To understand the implications of differences in approach here, from a knowledge-intensive firm's perspective, it is best to analyze the process from the client's perspective.

When the client purchases the services of a knowledge-intensive firm, thereby opening its doors to external consultants, it is inadvertently signaling to both its superiors and inferiors that the organization has reached a point where it needs help. This shows both vulnerability and strength, while revealing important information about the organization.

Of course, consultancy is not something that is sought only when an organization has a major problem that it is unable to address on its own. Seeking help should not suggest a weakness. On the contrary, consulting is often applied to *boost* client competences and capacity, perhaps as a result of rapid growth or a strategic change of focus. The requirement may take the form of help with a strategy project, supplementary resources for an internal IT assignment, or a targeted solution for a particular legal situation.

The external service provider will need to be sensitive, however. Their presence in the client organization may not be well received by everyone. It may spark fear that jobs are at risk or that internal skills have been deemed inadequate, causing resentment and demotivation. Navigating their way into the client company will require special skills and qualities on the part of the professionals, if they are to ruffle the least amount of feathers.

On entering the client organization, external 'experts' may appear to have an air of superiority – for example, perhaps because of the language and specialist terminology they are using. Perhaps they have short-circuited hierarchical structures by talking to everybody. The incoming professionals are often highly visible, too, because they behave and dress differently and because they are responding to an expectation by the client that they are going to perform. The consultant has very little choice, then, but to be seen to rise to the task.

To be effective, consultants must understand what is at stake for the client in inviting external help into the organization. By seeing the situation through the client's eyes, and that of the organization's employees, the incoming professional is far better able to apply sensitivity and ensure that the internal teams involved will be most receptive and co-operative.

It is important that the consultant possesses the ability to understand the client's position, speak the client's language, and ideally acts from within the client premises. As Danish philosopher Søren Kierkegaard put it, back in

1859: 'In order to truly succeed in leading a person to a certain point, you must first and foremost find him where he is and start from there.'

Although this is obviously quite a simple statement, it is an approach that many consultancy firms and other knowledge-intensive organizations would do well to remember, even today. Being sensitive to the client's starting point, in the widest sense, is vitally important if the external solution provider is to create a relationship based on trust, which can contribute to building confidence and 'buy-in' from the client's managers and employees. Only that way can the professionals be assured of delivering what is really needed.

Establishing a trust-based relationship with a client is a long-term project; it is not something that comes automatically, no matter how strong the consultancy firm's reputation and track record. It is something that happens gradually, and which is earned over time. The team of incoming professionals would be well advised to invest time in nurturing the client, as trust and confidence are established and the relationship is bedded down. Part of this process involves persuading and showing the client that you are there for *their* sake – that *their* needs come first, not the consultant's needs (for a quick profit, for instance).

It is possible to apply some science to this. Maister *et al.*, authors of *The Trusted Advisor* (2000), have developed what they refer to as a 'confidence formula' (see Figure 7.2). This defines confidence as a function of the consultant's credibility, trustworthiness, and ability to step outside their own interests and priorities in order to do their best for the client. Maister *et al.*, deem this to be critical in earning the right to become a 'trusted advisor'. Without these qualities, someone who is highly credible and reliable may be viewed merely as a 'technician' if they don't also demonstrate some degree of intimacy – i.e. the ability to understand and sympathize with a client's circumstances.

The trust equation $T = \dfrac{C + R + I}{S}$

T = Trustworthiness
C = Credibility – words: 'I can trust what he says'
R = Reliability – actions: 'I can trust her in what she is doing'
I = Intimacy – feelings: 'I feel comfortable discussing this'
S = Self-orientation – motives: 'I can trust that he cares about'

FIGURE 7.2 Confidence formula

Being as open and transparent as possible is a big part of this. As long as knowledge-intensive firms attempt to blind their clients with science, there will be an element of fear and potentially mistrust. Although there may be a natural reticence to give away their competitive edge, professionals should be prepared to share rather than possessively guard their valuable knowledge. This applies during the sales process, too – not just once a sale has been agreed.

Too many knowledge-intensive firms believe that they can keep their knowledge and competence to themselves until the ink is dry on a contract, despite operating in the most transparent age ever! With the proliferation of the Internet globally; significant workforce mobility between knowledge-intensive firms, and between providers and clients; and a labor market where large volumes of people are highly educated, and where supplementary training and lifelong learning are a priority, it is incomprehensible that knowledge-intensive firms can get away with sending out the signal: 'I want to wring every last cent out of you, dear client. Buy me on the basis of unconfirmed promises. Then I will open the box and share my experience, while the meter is running.'

Instead, consultants should possess a sincere desire to develop the relationship towards a win-win situation. This means taking a genuine interest in the client and wanting them to succeed – i.e. caring about the outcome from *their* perspective.

Our belief is that open and direct knowledge-sharing pays off. No knowledge-intensive firms can hold on to their knowledge in the long run anyway. Sharing knowledge and upgrading clients for free are much more valuable to the client and afford more prestige to the firm. Rather than giving away the crown jewels, providing competitors and clients with access to proprietary methods and knowledge signals a profound wish to help the client; it also suggests a certain self-confidence – that the value the firm generates to its clients extends far beyond what can be documented on paper.

Tor Nørretranders, the Danish popular scientist and author of *What it Means to be Human*, uses the example of a peacock to illustrate this point. Why does the female peacock select the male with the most beautiful feathers, he asks, given that he will be the one most likely to be attacked by the tiger? It is because the qualities of the alpha male extend beyond the superficial – they also signal that the creature is in his prime, agile, and strong – and therefore capable of avoiding the tiger.

The same goes for knowledge-intensive firms with an open or even aggressive knowledge-sharing policy toward their clients. By laying their credentials on the line they are saying: 'We have nothing to fear from the competition; we are way ahead of them, and these skills and this experience are in our blood'.

Unfortunately, examples of such boldness are few and far between in consultancy markets.

Matching sales to strategy

Other factors will be at play, too, as professionals negotiate the sales process. Before they get too far into establishing trust and confidence, they will need to ensure, for example, that the client and the given project are a good fit for their organization. If the assignment does not align with the company strategy and business model, investing any further time in developing the dialog may be wasteful and misleading. The firm's strategy should function as a prism for the priorities needed in the sales effort, too. The basic questions to ask to assess how well the client and project match to the company strategy are those touched on in previous chapters – for example, whom do we want to deliver and therefore sell to, how, and with what competences?

This, in turn, should determine how the firm prioritizes its sales effort. Every time you choose to pursue a client or a new project lead, you will be turning down the chance to use those same resources in other opportunities. Avoiding a clash with potentially more profitable or otherwise more fruitful projects means having an awareness of what constitutes the best kind of business for your firm, and what this looks like in a sales situation.

Sales opportunities may present themselves in different ways, either through competitive tender scenarios or by more discrete networking and word of mouth – perhaps the result of a previous engagement with the same client or where a client contact has moved to another company and now needs the firm's services again. The target market, the level of competition found in it, and the particular types of services you provide, may all have a bearing on the way your firm focusses its sales efforts.

The competitive situation of knowledge-intensive firms is often determined by the market. Specifically, by:

- client preferences;
- the volume and nature of clients in the market; and
- the knowledge-intensive firm's strategy as concerns the competitive markets it wants to play in.

TABLE 7.1 Markets for knowledge-intensive firms

	Competition	Relations
Existing clients	Competition market – firms with strong competitiveness	Key account management
New clients	Broad marketing and canvassing	Network based

Table 7.1 illustrates how the market situation for knowledge-intensive firms is configured.

Client development strategy

Just as knowledge-intensive firms select their own markets, clients will determine the way they procure services and therefore how sales will need to be approached.

The supply of firms will be a contributing factor to the competitive situation, as is the decision of clients whether to invite tenders or award an assignment to a specific supplier without competition. Public sector knowledge-intensive firms will choose their markets to a degree, too – that is, they will have some say in how they segment their client base when it comes to who will receive which kind of service (and how quickly, with how much resources, and through which type of interventions, etc.).

In markets with low-entry barriers, there is likely to be a large supply of knowledge-intensive firms with services that are relatively easy to sell. Low-entry barriers could include the following:

- A lack of industry or legal regulation, education or certification, or requirements for membership of given associations allowing you to practice.
- Only a moderate need for investment when establishing a knowledge-intensive firm. This can apply in industries such as consulting, public relations, and communication, where the primary capital is the professionals and their competences – so that all it takes to be in business is a computer and a phone.
- Scenarios where the demand for specially developed methods and technology is not particularly strong.

- Situations where a backlash against the high fees of competing players has created a new opportunity for entry-level services with a more affordable price tag.

Some clients favor a scenario where there is competition and adhere to the principle that tenders should be invited from a large or small group of knowledge-intensive firms. They may want to exert price pressure or test the quality or the innovation in the market. Perhaps they want to court variety or at least ensure that variety remains in the market – i.e. that a single knowledge-intensive firm is not able to achieve too dominant a position. Or there may be more formal reasons for the need to go out to tender – particularly in the public sector, where this is the only sure way to secure (or be seen to secure) 'best value for money', and to guard against underhand practices.

Other clients prefer to engage the stick with what they know, utilizing the same partner in multiple assignments on the basis that, if a relationship is working well, why rock the boat by introducing a less well-known entity? Also, by broadening a single relationship, the client may hope to benefit from discounted fees.

Equally, it could be that the knowledge-provider is one of only a handful of specialists in its field, and unique, or the market leader, in its particular combination of skills and experience for that target market. Or perhaps so much has been invested in the relationship, establishing a history, trust, and confidence, that starting again with a new provider, just for the sake of shaking things up, getting a fresh perspective, and renegotiating on price, would not be worth it or would even be risky.

Knowing its target market, the knowledge-intensive firm must prioritize its sales activities accordingly, making sure they are always considered in situations where tenders are invited or are the first to hear about new opportunities in closed situations.

Non-competitive opportunities are particularly attractive to knowledge-intensive firms because the cost of sale is lower. Formal tendering is labor-intensive, incurring a cost each time a bid is not won, while fewer resources will be invested in the development of the contract in a non-competitive scenario because it will not be necessary to address all aspects of the challenge in order to build as strong a proposal as possible.

For these reasons, it is attractive to many knowledge-intensive firms to develop proactively close relationships with their clients, thus ensuring not only that they become the obvious first port of call when a new situation arises (ideally avoiding a competitive situation, where this is permitted), but also that they are the first to hear about it, giving them an advantage if they are later required to bid for the work. This approach can also lead to word-of-mouth recommendations, both within a client organization and in affiliated and partner operations, or as a particular client contact moves to another firm.

Knowledge-intensive firms which rely on a high proportion of sales to new clients will have an acute need to influence and network in this way. Word-of-mouth recommendations are shown to be by far the most powerful marketing tool next to the relationally determined – where the consultant is involved in the continual nurturing of the client relationship.

Anders Lavesen, partner at the leading Scandinavian law firm Kromann Reumert, describes his firm's sales approach as comprising 80 percent 'farming' and 20 percent 'hunting', mostly in relation to medium-size companies. He says:

> Typically the client comes to us, but now and then we get invited to 'beauty contests'. The client's choice of lawyer is often based to a great extent on a preference for a particular individual. We could obviously win a few more clients if we were more outgoing, but the culture in our market suits us well and our sales are on the rise.

Proactive networking could add to this success, however, Lavesen concedes:

> We should all try to copy those of our lawyers who are more outgoing in terms of sales, and those who are more visible in their networks. Horse shows, tennis tournaments, receptions, etc., are good networking platforms. The outgoing lawyers are on the list when a client needs to select a lawyer.

There aren't many clients who take out advertisements in *The Financial Times* and *Wall Street Journal* to thank the firms they have worked with, but that is precisely what Independent Franchise Partners LLP did in August 2009 in recognition of the help it had received in setting up its business.

Prior to founding the new firm, founder and partner Hassan Elmasry had been managing director and lead portfolio manager for global and American franchise portfolios at Morgan Stanley Investment Management. In his new business, he was not going to have the luxury of Morgan Stanley's infrastructure and needed support to fill the gap. As a consultancy firm, Navigant was an obvious port of call, thanks to its specialist investment management team.

The brief was simple on paper: to help define Franchise Partners' business model, developing the specific requirements for it and implementing them. Navigant's integral involvement made all the difference between success and failure in these early, critical months for Franchise Partners: it now has a robust operating model and a base from which to grow its business.

Navigant also helped steer an outsourcing deal with a third party, Northern Trust, which is completely scalable, increasing in line with the client's business and providing flexibility so Franchise Partners can move into new areas if and when they want to, yet without increasing its own headcount significantly.

The expertise of the Navigant team played a critical role in winning its client's trust. Yet achieving Franchise Partners' goals was possible only because Elmasry and colleagues were willing to work with Navigant on a completely collaborative basis and to take decisions quickly.

Graham Macken, Managing Director at Navigant Consulting, describes the development of the client relationship: 'Throughout the project, all the key partners would sit around the table with us, listen to the options and our views, and make a decision then and there. A large, established organization would have found it very hard to move that fast.' The respect is mutual, says Hassan Elmasry, Managing Director and Lead Portfolio Manager for global and American franchise portfolios, Morgan Stanley Investment Management: 'There were occasions when we would have been hard-pushed to come up with a solution for a particular operational problem, but Navigant were never fazed; they always had a way forward. We felt we could completely trust their judgement.'

Andrew Stewart, Head of Financial Services Consulting in Europe at Navigant, comments:

> Projects such as this illustrate just how important relationships are in professional service. Relationships are important to us in two fundamental ways. The best consulting work can only take place where there's a good personal relationship between the client and consulting teams. Personal chemistry and the willingness to go the extra mile to ensure success are fundamental here. But relationships matter, too, at a corporate level. Much of our work comes from existing clients who are pleased with what we've achieved for them that far and trust us to do good work for them in the future.

Relationships matter in the public sector, too, even where they're not a source of revenue. Says Angie Brayshaw, Head of Employee Engagement at the UK's Department for Work and Pensions:

There are interesting dynamics here about who perceives who as the client. For people working on the front line, perhaps in Job Centre Plus offices, a client is someone who comes in looking for help. They may not want to be one of our clients, so that's one kind of relationship. For policy people, the important relationship is between them and the minister they ultimately work for, or between them and tax-payers, depending on where they sit in the organization. That's why, when we talk about our values, we have to illustrate them differently for different groups of people; we have to manage each of these sets of relationships quite differently.

Public sector departments responsible for internal delivery units (for example, HR and cost/salary administration) note that client satisfaction is becoming increasingly important in the government sector, as the front-line operations being 'served' begin to see themselves as 'customers'.

Since establishing the Danish State Financial Service Center, a single central shared-service unit, Director Sune Stausholm has found that the ministries it serves now demand a greater level of service than when each ministry had its own in-house staff:

> We have seen examples where client ministries now suddenly cannot live with deadlines that were in place before. When you do not manage something yourself, you accept less. We are in a client-provider relationship so we will see a lot of this. It is healthy, because it creates dialog and ensures that expectations are aligned. I am very business focussed and believe we must do things as well as we can within agreed pricing.

The decision over whether to focus on repeat sales to existing clients, versus courting new business, is one that each knowledge-intensive firm must make for itself, based on its particular market, strategy, and business model. Of course, the two approaches are not mutually exclusive, though an element of prioritization may be prudent to make best use of resources and to ensure that incoming business is well chosen, profitable, and fitting for the firm's brand profile and onward development.

Return on investment: prioritizing sales and marketing activity

When choosing a particular sales strategy, it is important to consider the effectiveness of each type of sale. Basically, the knowledge-intensive firm can adopt a sales strategy focussing on continuously aiming at new clients or targeting existing clients.

Focussing on bringing new clients in demands a certain sales strategy of expanded view on potential sales, whereas focussing on bringing new business in from existing clients demands investing in the relationship with existing clients. Thus, various competences are also needed from managers and professionals of knowledge-intensive firms depending on the strategy adopted.

To hunt or to farm?

While hedging all bets is attractive to ensure that no opportunity is missed, firms who spread themselves too thin, by trying to cover all bases, may live to regret it. Far better to do one job well than several jobs badly. The latter approach is likely to be costly and ultimately unprofitable, while resulting in a loss of strategic focus.

Management must choose, then, between a primary focus of sales resources on 'hunting', versus a concentration on 'farming'. Knowledge-intensive firms with a strong focus on existing clients are 'farmers', while those with a focus on generating new clients are 'hunters'. That said, all knowledge-intensive firms will need to retain a touch of the 'hunter' about them, so that new clients can be found to replace accounts that are lost or which currently lie dormant. New client relationships will also need to be created to sustain growth.

Hunters

Knowledge-intensive firms of the hunter type are constantly seeking out new prey – i.e. new clients who want to purchase their services. There is often a strong dynamism in such organizations because the constant pursuit demands adrenalin, commitment to the awareness of new market opportunities, and the will to pursue leads.

Incentive structures in knowledge-intensive firms with a focus on new business may be geared toward rewarding the *sale* more highly than the subsequent delivery of the solution. Star performers may be lonely wolves with strong personal characteristics and clout among clients, or they may take young apprentices under their wing who can support them with research and by preparing tenders. In a market rife with competition, the killer instinct of such personalities will be a highly prized asset.

This being the case, the knowledge-intensive firm will need to recruit professionals who derive great satisfaction from creating quick results and settling contracts. Hunters are constantly on the look-out for new opportunities; they do not linger to survey the territory. If there is no potential in a lead, they move on quickly, keen not to waste time or resources.

The hunter organization will divide the market into many groups of clients. The hunters are allocated huge client segment responsibility (large hunting grounds), calling for a constant focus on scouting for new clients. The strategy is often focussed on a broad portfolio. The philosophy will often be to 'shoot at anything that moves'. If this is not the firm's official strategy, it will often over-rule a strategy with a narrower focus on the market in which the knowledge-intensive firm should operate. Some knowledge-intensive firms with a hunter profile will also be able to operate with a tight strategy. This will typically be firms that sell concrete concept-based services. For this reason, there will be a limited market for their services, while the market will be broadly defined in terms of the potential client group.

Among the challenges facing the hunter organizations is the risk of neglecting existing clients as soon as a sale has been realized. Conflicts may also arise between the efficient salesperson who is seen to be greatly rewarded for the 'win', and the colleagues who subsequently have to produce the service – yet who may feel that, in so doing, they are failing to achieve equivalent status or recognition.

Farmers

Knowledge-intensive firms with a primary focus on *existing* clients are known as farmers. They cultivate and farm their soil, and their expectations in terms of benefits are realized over a longer timeframe. They invest in each relationship and contribute something here and now which in the longer term will translate into profits.

While there is not necessarily a lack of dynamic initiative in this type of knowledge-intensive firm, but rather an acceptance that production and the nurturing of client relationships take time, this set-up demands a certain patience when it comes to seeing results. Here, the adrenalin will be generated by actively servicing existing clients in concrete tasks, as well as through an extension of the relationship into new areas as new needs present themselves. The vigilant gaze in this case, then, is to a lesser extent focussed on *new* market opportunities and rather primarily directed at the existing clients' needs and how you can fulfill these as a farmer. The priority is not to *sell* here and now, but rather to *help* — based on a philosophy that the trusted helper will be rewarded in time, when a new need arises.

Incentive structures in firms with a focus on existing clients tend to focus on reward for the maintenance of the client relationship. Here, a dedication to hard work on the long run has status; it is attractive to be appointed key account manager with responsibility for important clients.

Knowledge-intensive firms with a focus on client relations emphasize the good performance of an assignment, recognizing that unique, high-quality solutions are the most important drivers in the maintenance of a client relationship, which then continues to generate repeat business through additional assignments. Trust is vital here, too. This can be achieved or enhanced through unselfish action, where the service provider goes the extra mile to assist the client with issues that are important to them, even if this does not lead to additional payment in the short term.

At global accounting firm KPMG, the sensitive handling of client relationships is paramount to ongoing success. Technical knowledge and commitment are both passports to a deeper, more personal relationship, which necessitates taking the long view:

> You become a sounding board: clients will pick up the phone and bounce issues off you. It's not something clients ever really pay for, but they get a lot of value from it. At the end of the day, we're into long-term relationships — these are going to be what we live and die by. And that's what clients want too. They want to know that, when the chips are down, they can come to an individual whom they know and trust, and say, 'Can you sort it, please?' — top executive at KPMG.

The stars in farmer organizations will be empathic professionals who have an ability to establish close client relationships that will support the firm through many years via a continual influx of new assignments. This can be hard work, especially if it means persuading the rest of the organization to prioritize allocation of the best resources, the best services, and the best discounts to a given client.

Success in this sales approach will depend on attracting professionals who derive great job satisfaction from devoting patient attention to client relationships, and from delivering good service with a view to long-term benefits. If clients are satisfied over time, they will keep returning, forging a still closer relationship where the consultant is a party to even more information with the client.

In this way, the farmer is just as busy as the hunter. A proportion of their work hours is spent on service and relationship-building that cannot be invoiced, while other tasks are attended to, and concrete sales and development assignments taken care of.

A farmer organization will tend to segment the market into individual clients. A central tool is the key account managers, who are awarded responsibility for individual clients who need in-depth attention. These professionals will need to develop relationships at all levels of the organization, get to know still more clients in the organization, make themselves useful, and build ever deeper trust in these firms.

As is to be expected, relationship-building strategies are vulnerable to the loss of clients, because each account represents a major investment built up over many years. It takes a long time to develop new clients. To allow for this, knowledge-intensive firms in this category must spread their risk by cultivating a number of in-depth client relationships, and by ensuring high quality in *every* delivery, so that no client becomes tempted to look for alternative providers.

The strategy of farmer organizations is often based on a quite targeted market. Their philosophy should be *not* to suggest that they are world champions at everything or that they are better than they actually are. Creating unrealistic expectations will disappoint and undermine trust, threatening the long-term potential of fledgling relationships and negatively affecting the company's standing in the market. In any event, knowledge-intensive organizations claiming to be able to handle everything are more likely to be sending out the message that they are actually not world champions at anything specific.

Conflict can arise in farmer organizations where professionals specializing in a particular service believe that colleagues servicing other markets do not deliver the same level of quality, which risks damaging the company brand. When colleagues holding other specialist competences move into a given client account, there may be doubts that these team members do not understand the complexity of the given assignment, or the particular client's needs and preferences. Such conflicts can arise in even quite small organizations, if there are diverse areas of specialization involved.

Solutions to such issues can be found in knowledge-sharing, co-ordination, and sensitive management, all of which are valuable tools in ensuring a uniform quality level and in creating a mutual understanding among professionals of how the firm works – including the necessity of cross-disciplinary co-operation. If professionals can learn to accept and trust each other when introducing colleagues into jealously guarded accounts, they will find that the resulting collaboration increases efficiency.

Key account management and the road to intimacy

Clearly, not all clients can be given the same attention and priority. It is expensive to spend non-billable time on clients, even if long-term goals make going the extra mile seem worth it, so knowledge-intensive firms will need to select carefully the clients that qualify for more systematic attention and development. Such clients are typically labeled 'key accounts'. Many firms appoint key account managers or partners who are responsible for the development of client contact and the co-ordination of the firm's work for and relations with the client.

Servicing priority clients

A central aspect of key account management is to handle the client relationship professionally and consciously, while ensuring that the client's preferences are observed. The client should experience added value through extra attention. When choosing between client satisfaction or profitability in performing the assignment, the needs of the client should be given the highest priority. The signal to the client should always be that the knowledge-intensive firm is keen to invest in the long-term relationship, and that it sees this as more important than any short-term profit to the firm.

As we have already discussed, establishing a trust-based relationship with the client means that the knowledge-intensive firm gains access to higher levels of the value chain in the client organization. The more critical an assignment is to the client, the more they will be inclined to assign the task to a trusted partner, as opposed to inviting tenders and risking choosing an inferior company. The more important a task is to a client, the more the client will be inclined to pay well for the solution, too, again to minimize any risks of a less than optimum delivery. For all these reasons, it is attractive for the knowledge-intensive firm to have an influence and to operate at the highest possible level in the client's value chain.

Client reputation as a driver

Selecting which clients should be awarded 'key account' status is a strategic decision based on the fit of the client to the company strategy, target market, and business model. The future potential of the client in representing additional work and profits will be another important consideration. Or perhaps the client's name is prestigious and will look good to other prospects. Maybe they represent a chance to deliver a high degree of innovation, making the client attractive to work with, as a means of keeping professionals motivated, and in developing new experience that can later be exploited for the benefit of other clients.

Key account management applies in the public sector just as much as in the private sector, as is highlighted by the observations of Lotte Grünbaum, former Head of Corporate HR at the Center for Corporate Administration at the Danish Ministry of the Environment:

> We can learn a lot from private management consulting firms: how to handle clients and key accounts. Although there is much hype about this discipline, it does have value. It could mean simply visiting clients to discuss how the service and co-operation should be. It is important to have ambassadors who promote us to others, that we are well connected. Client satisfaction is the highest among clients we know and have a relationship with. In a distanced relation, it is easy to end up with a 'them and us' culture.

It is one thing to go the extra mile for a client, but this must be in an area which adds genuine value for them, so that these measures are appreciated fully as an investment in a good long-term relationship. Client care is often characterized by a tangible presence during the process of co-operation, which helps and supports the client. It can be small details like this that help distinguish the services of one firm from those of a competitor.

Special measures deemed to be of value might include a high degree of flexibility: the ability to provide additional analyses when needed, perhaps at short notice; meeting a tight deadline that has suddenly arisen; helping the client to develop a presentation; or keeping the client informed about subjects of interest – demonstrating that you are still thinking about the client when doing something else.

Some knowledge-intensive firms also find it beneficial to tell their clients when they should *not* buy the services of the company, either because they are too expensive or because other knowledge-intensive firms have more relevant competence for a given assignment. Such honesty creates good will, while demonstrating that you have put the client's needs before your own.

But, again, it is important to choose key accounts carefully, as it will be impossible – and unprofitable – to extend such high levels of attention to every client account.

Thought-leadership as a brand booster

Another way to impress clients and boost the relationship with them is to position the firm as a 'thought leader' – that is, a firm which is identified by clients as having a leading competence in a particular field. Thought leaders are typically major players in a particular industry, but they can also be small, highly specialized firms that have won this position in a particular area through high levels of expertise. Often such status is achieved by excellent professional skills and through extraordinary marketing activities via publications, conferences, study tours, and so on. Becoming a thought leader creates a strong professional brand that is hard to beat competitively.

In a world with increasing market transparency and knowledge exchange, it is even more appealing to knowledge-intensive firms to develop activities that might establish them as thought leaders in core markets. The Internet, for one, serves as a fantastic showcase for thought-leadership content – white papers and discussion documents, webinars, and so on, all designed to 'educate' potential clients, while subtly driving them into the firm's arms by reinforcing the perception that they know the most, or the very latest, about a given market, discipline, or approach.

Consequently, many knowledge-intensive firms allocate a lot of resources to value-creating marketing. Here, they take their accumulated knowledge, generated via assignments, perhaps adding to this with perspectives developed though analytical activities. This combined knowledge is then disseminated via newsletters, articles, and analytical reports on a given industry or a certain phenomenon, even through the publication of books written by professionals in the company, establishing them and the firm as cutting-edge specialists in a given field.

Strong firms tend to be those that are the most generous in – and the least afraid of – making their competences available for everybody. They see a market value in demonstrating that they have no problem sharing their knowledge (often on their websites) because neither clients nor competitors can steal a concept and derive the same value from it as the firm itself.

Particularly dedicated employees at McKinsey & Company publish professional articles in *McKinsey Quarterly*, for example. Accenture, meanwhile, has its own think-tanks – Accenture Institute for High Performance Business and Accenture Institute for Public Service Value – established for the purpose of gathering knowledge and disseminating and marketing it – for instance, through the company's publications, *Outlook* and *The Point*. IBM, too, has an electronic newsletter, *IdeaWatch: Business Perspectives from IBM Global Business Services*.

Research presents a similar opportunity to trumpet the firm's knowledge. Here, for example, recurring research, financed by the firm and perhaps sponsors is used to demonstrate the firm's substantial knowledge in a particular area. Global IT analyst firm, Gartner Group, is very good at this.

Less resource-consuming alternatives may include short seminars, perhaps held during a morning or afternoon where clients are invited to meet a couple of speakers – typically someone from the firm, as well as an independent outsider or client. The firm imparts its knowledge and conveys its expertise, subliminally promoting its credentials, while the prospective clients walk away having learnt something and having made new contacts – seemingly for 'free'.

Paid trips or study tours, where perhaps clients are invited to certain high-performing organizations or to attend an event, can also be valuable in securing sales and building strong client relationships. This approach requires that clients can accept such offers – or pay the full price themselves. (Public sector clients are generally unable to accept such financed arrangements.) The pharmaceutical industry has honed this particular art, inviting doctors to professional conferences. These are often staged in geographically exciting places or combined with exciting off-agenda activities to boost the attraction of attending. IT consultancies also use study tours for clients as a means to develop networks.

Summary

In this chapter we have explored the way sales approaches and activities, and after-sales client relationship development, must be aligned with the strategy of the knowledge-intensive firm, since it is during the sales process that the firm will decide which assignments to focus on, and therefore the profile it wants to create in the market.

We have seen the importance of trust in selling knowledge-intensive solutions, given that the end product with such firms is hard to demonstrate, and because the impact will be different for each client. Professionals involved in the sale must therefore be able to promote excellent professional skills and have the ability to handle sensitively the individual client, as well as their particular interaction requirements as the relationship develops.

As we have noted, sales can take the 'hunting' or the 'farming' strategy of either aiming at bringing new clients in or focussing on developing business with existing clients. Various competences are needed to succeed with each strategy. 'Farming' builds upon key account management to ensure that hard-won clients remain loyal, and that new business can be derived from elsewhere in the organization, and from higher in the client's value chain.

Other strategies for influencing client choices include value-added activities such as 'thought leadership' positioning, though this requires an investment of time and resources, and necessitates that the company is comfortable and confident about sharing its knowledge without fear of compromising their competitive advantage.

Questions for reflection

- Is your firm a hunter organization, applying fairly extensive resources to the cultivation of new clients, and shooting at almost everything that moves; or a farmer organization which devotes the majority of its sales resources to nurturing and furthering existing relationships?
- How does this favored approach fit with your broader company strategy?
- Does the firm attempt to establish itself as a thought leader in strategic key markets? If so, does the firm invest sufficiently in achieving thought-leadership status? Is there more you could be doing?
- Where is your firm positioned on a scale from 1 to 10 (where 1 is inferior and 10 superior) in terms of applying the 'trust' formula in the firm's sales activities?

8
HOLISTIC MANAGEMENT: THE PYRAMID AT PLAY

In this penultimate chapter, it is time to draw together the various themes we have unraveled throughout this book to determine what optimum interplay between the different dimensions of the knowledge-intensive management pyramid should look like (Figure 8.1).

In the chapters so far, we have taken various challenges of management in turn, examining how each affects and applies to knowledge-intensive firms — and how approaches can be optimized to maximize results. Clearly, however, management cannot be effected on a discreet basis, focussing

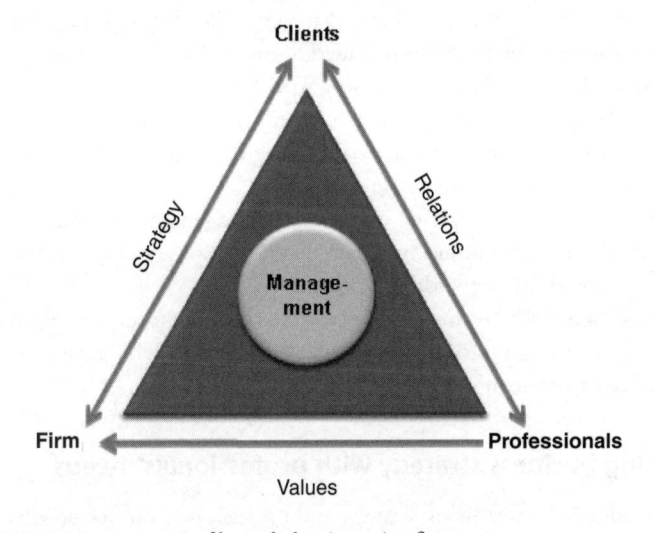

FIGURE 8.1 Management of knowledge-intensive firms

on each factor in turn, in isolation. Day-to-day situations and challenges make for a much muddier picture, where successful steering of the business demands an agreed overall vision, clear guidelines, and good intentions, complemented by commonsense and pragmatic action which strikes the best balance in each set of circumstances.

As we noted at the beginning of this journey, for the knowledge-intensive firm effective management is about balancing the needs and priorities of the organization itself with those of its clients and its professionals through the company strategy, business model, and values; staff recruitment and development approach; client relationship focus; and supporting processes and systems.

This chapter considers how all this can be brought together harmoniously and with maximum positive impact for the firm, its valued professionals, and the target client base.

Management in knowledge-intensive firms takes place on different levels:

- organizational and technological;
- value based; and
- client.

Organizational and technological management concerns the ability of a firm to model and structure the organization efficiently. This begins with establishing a convincing strategy, founded on a strong business model and supported by good systems.

Value-based management is executed through the ability to take the lead and be a role model to professionals. Through cultural modeling of the organization, management's preferences to actions and culture are instilled in and accepted among professionals, so being executed in the professionals' daily decisions in client-handling, performance in assignments, sales, internal communication with colleagues, and so on.

Client management is carried out via the management's interaction with clients, as manifested through manager–client relations, and more generally in sales presentations, networking, and so on.

To have an impact on an everyday basis, all these management approaches need to carry through into strategic action – i.e. actions which have strategic significance to the firm's development.

Balancing business strategy with professionals' needs

In knowledge-intensive firms, strategy and professionals cannot be separated as they presuppose each other. It is this underlying fact that makes knowledge-intensive firms so interesting and yet challenging to manage. Many competences are at play, and managers are continuously challenged by professionals because they are experts in their fields, with a strong desire to have an influence over the work they do and how they do this. Ambitious professionals will thus be keen to contribute to and qualify strategy development, personnel policy, sales decisions, etc.

Professionals are essential to the development of a knowledge-intensive firm, and they know it. This is true in both the short and long term. The best managers are adept at handling professionals to get the most out of them for the benefit of the firm. In a win-win situation, this will be achieved in such a way the professionals also get the best out of the company, in terms of development of their professional and personal skills, thereby growing their own market value.

Company development must be directed by an over-riding company strategy, but there should also be a certain pragmatism to act strategically according to high-value opportunities. For example, this may mean establishing a new branch to the organization in response to the desire of a star professional to move to another country or city, who is able to convince the management to support this request through company expansion.

This is how London-based consulting firm Matrix branched into Washington, DC, in 2008 – because one of the partners wanted to move to the US. The establishment of an American office was one way of preventing this partner from leaving the company, while also benefiting from his longing to go abroad. Likewise, this was how Rambøll Management Consulting branched into Germany in 2000 – because the right conditions suddenly came about and were pursued pragmatically, even though the company had a Scandinavian expansion strategy. Knowledge-intensive firms abound with such anecdotes.

In short, professionals are the capital of the knowledge-intensive firm. Where the output is a service that has been tailored to a greater or lesser extent to the needs of the client, the makeup and quality of that output are inherently linked to and dependent on the professionals themselves – the knowledge, skills, and experience they represent and the way that they work. Without them, there would be no firm, or business.

It would be easy to argue, then, that professionals are more important than strategy. They are decisive to the development of the business, after all, since the firm's development occurs via engaged, motivated, and competent professionals. Yet without a strategy to guide them in their choices, professionals could run amok, leaving chaos in their wake. For this reason, others counter that strategy must always come first, just as it does in other markets. Without a strategy there would be no guidance about which markets, clients, and types of business to target, how, and based on which business model. The result could be a loss of focus, badly managed resources, suboptimal profits, weakened client relationships, and a less stable position in the market.

If the upshot is a chicken-and-egg argument about which should come first, the strategy or the professional, the only practical conclusion can be that the two are interdependent, so that neither can function well without reference to – and reverence for – the other. The knowledge-intensive firm should neither flow opportunistically with the preferences of the professionals, then, nor flow freely with the market. Instead, there must be agreed boundaries, and flexibility within them, on both sides.

Strategy establishes direction, defines guidelines, and defines boundaries not to be crossed. Professionals, meanwhile, create energy, drive, enthusiasm, and results. In knowledge-intensive firms, it is the employees' daily passion and motivated work that drive the business. However, this is not sufficient. The firm and the professionals must have a strategic outlook to direct and balance spontaneous passions and opportunistic preferences.

Cultural modeling comes into play here. The management of cultural modeling of the organization is the basis on which strategy and professionals interact; it is the basis for establishing shared values upon which management and professionals are guided in their daily behavior and the decisions they make.

Another consideration when it comes to the interplay of different management challenges and goals is the needs of individual professionals and the extent to which these match – or can be engineered to match – the development goals of the firm. If the professionals are not on board with the direction the firm is taking and the types of assignments it takes on, key staff may leave with the result that any business development stalls. Knowledge-intensive firms should aim to develop with full awareness of professionals' competences and preferences, then – to the extent that these can be accommodated within the agreed company strategy.

Fulfilling the need to make a difference

As we have seen in previous chapters, professionals in knowledge-intensive fields tend to be ambitious, seeking personal as well as career fulfillment in the work they do. Give them mundane, routine work and their enthusiasm may wane; throw them in the deep end without support and they may feel their confidence and reputation is being threatened. A key challenge in retaining high performers, then, is to match assignments to their skills and ambitions, wherever possible, giving them maximum opportunity to learn, hone, perfect, stretch, and shine. They will seek out new challenges to push themselves, welcoming the chance to innovate, and be recognized for what they have achieved. Look over their shoulders, and they may feel they are being 'supervised'. Look away too long and they may feel overlooked and unappreciated.

Professionals in knowledge-intensive firms are motivated by feeling that they make a difference. After a decade, they want to be able to look back at the time they spent with a knowledge-intensive firm and see that they created change – that they were part of something big, that they made a difference.

Agnete Gersing, Director at the Danish Competition Authority, confirms the need to motivate professionals by creating 'meaning' in the work they do, from a public sector perspective:

> We are privileged in that the solutions we produce to most people seem naturally meaningful. They are beneficial to society. We mainly employ economists and lawyers. They typically have a professional background, where they have already worked with aspects of competition. Hence the task of explaining why the assignment is meaningful is relatively easy.
>
> In the public sector, you receive money to solve certain problems assigned to the institution. We focus on approaches that create effects to the benefit of society. Having a critical approach to the type of assignment you take on can be important to the employees. Motivating them requires a combination of several approaches. We must justify our existence transparently and communicate our purpose at any given occasion; clarify the interesting aspects of the individual assignment and the effect it will create; be clear about the concrete work people do, so they can see that they make a difference.

The balancing act from a management perspective, then, is to manage proactively without being seen to supervise, and to be able to hand out new challenges fairly, and in a way that doesn't compromise the quality of the delivery or the profitability of the assignment (for example, if senior personnel are being allocated inappropriately).

Shelia Evans-Tranumn, Associate Commissioner at the New York State Department of Education (DOE), where she spent 16 years until retirement in the spring of 2010, claims that, while she found managing people not especially difficult over the years, it did require a lot of time. Being in the public sector posed its own challenges, too, she notes:

> It is the level of intensity that is needed. Here in America, we are generally under-funded in terms of staffing needs. 12–14 hour days are common for a leader. The leaders of big corporations make sure that they can have clothes delivered to them, so when they pull those all-nighters they've got something clean to change into at the end of it. And you see those black Lincoln town cars outside of corporate offices, so they bring you home for four hours of sleep, and they would pay for your meal.
>
> The public sector is different: I had to drive myself and pay for my own food! Yet, I had to drive my people as hard as you'd drive people in the private sector, but without these tools. So we have to do things differently. I had to create a culture of: 'We have to get this work done by six o'clock. I want to find out when your children get home, and if it is five o'clock, I will see if I can have you to go home by five, and then you can go on the computer at night when they are asleep.'

When she first joined the department, there wasn't much thought given to the needs of professionals when planning strategy or work, so Evans-Tranumn had to take radical action to turn things around. She says:

> When I arrived, this was a massive bureaucracy. People were hired for various reasons, some because they'd been unsuccessful in schools; others were researchers who just wanted to write about education. I came with a new vision and energy – and they thought I was crazy. They knew they hadn't been hired to do the work I now wanted them to do.
>
> I had to start with what I had: I had to assess their skills and see who I could get to do which jobs. I needed to tap in on some unhidden resources that each person brought to the table, so I talked to them on what their passions were outside their jobs and discovered that they did some interesting things. As a result, we found people who had competences in their private lives which we could make use of. There was, for example, someone who was interested in and good at making television programs, so we converted that hobby into a television show promoting education.
>
> Our next step was a reorganization so that we could get some people out and some new people in. We didn't need to shed a lot of

people – just a few – but we did need to publicize the fact we were prepared to do this, so everyone else could figure out that they'd need to shape up. At the same time, I got the state legislature to agree that my office needed new people – something that meant being creative and savvy enough to understand how to get more positions even in a hard time. We also had to be clear about what we were looking for.

Although a good salary can help, where there is the budget to go beyond the market rate, money alone will not ensure that professionals commit and are sufficiently motivated. For long-term fulfillment and to ensure innovation and added value, professionals require an inspiring working environment – with good management, good colleagues, and good clients.

Leaders, like Evans-Tranumn, must be capable of creating enthusiasm, inspiring, and motivating professionals; they must be prepared and able to establish attractive goals, concepts, and guidelines in ways that stimulate their employees. We refer to this as 'motivation-based management' – i.e. ensuring a development via commitment and creative drive.

Motivation-based management can be executed collectively as well as on an individual basis in the relationship with each professional. Collectively, this takes place at staff meetings, seminars, and so on. These are appropriate forums during which goals and guidelines can be consolidated and enthusiasm created. However, the most substantial way of create meaning and enthusiasm is through individual relationships, where the manager attempts to motivate each person based on their own unique terms, via particular assignments. In this situation, the manager can create real dedication.

Providing a development path

Proactively mentoring and coaching professionals is another way of developing them so that they feel special and stay interested, and so that they 'grow' in line with the strategic development goals of the business.

Mentoring

We define mentoring as the matching of a senior professional with a more junior colleague on an operational assignment, to support the younger team member's development. This can happen in more or less structured ways, but an important aspect of mentoring is that it takes place here and now, allowing real learning to happen on the job. Cumulative feedback given six months later in a performance appraisal might not be perceived by the professional as having practical, positive value. Rather, it may be considered a punishment, without the immediate possibility of correcting their actions or otherwise demonstrating an improvement.

Mentoring could be something as simple as commenting on a memo, report, or presentation, thereby helping the professional to improve, or it could be feedback on a professional's performance during a client presentation. This appraisal might take place in the car on the way home from a meeting with a client or in the office.

With our combined 50 years in management and management research, the authors of this book have witnessed visible development by knowledge-intensive firms in this area. Young professionals make considerably greater demands today, when it comes to their competence development and feedback. They are very conscious of the fact that they only develop through continuous, honest feedback, so this is something they now crave.

Anders Lavesen, partner at leading Scandinavian law firm Kromann Reumert, agrees that personnel management should be implemented with a focus on the individual. He says:

> Personnel management is about attention, coaching, and the role as professional advisor: coaching people with regard to their development. All the things involved in personal education should be discussed every day. We should become better at delegating, and better at following up and spending time on this afterwards. Those who are most successful in this company are also those who are best at this. The competences you develop in your management behavior toward the employees also develop your ability to interact with the clients.

Coaching

Coaching, on the other hand, supports professionals' reflections on their own performance, results, and development. It takes its point of departure in concrete assignments performed and the professional's ambitions for development.

Some maintain that coaching only takes effect if it is given in a neutral way – i.e. in a space where the existing authority relationship is phased out during the coaching. However, we do not think this is possible. If a manager maintains that they are capable of moving in and out of the coaching relationship with the professional without any prejudice and authority, this could signal low credibility. The words spoken during a coaching conversation will not be forgotten or transformed, no matter how professionally the manager and the professional intend to act.

If both parties realize that coaching is a management tool, coaching can become a strong means for the development of professionals. As coach, the manager can apply their insight and strategic preferences to assist the professionals in realizing their roles and opportunities, and finding focus areas to ensure they get the desired development in areas significant to the company.

Management consultants at the Danish management consultancy Attractor (part of the Rambøll Group) confirm the need for a systematic approach to professional development:

> 'The management coach must in quite undramatic ways create transparency with regard to the quality of relations at play between manager and employee,' one comments. 'The employee is hired to solve a set of problems, yet it is the management's responsibility that the problems are solved in the best possible ways. The coaching, from the manager's point of view, should support the organizational functionality and logic – i.e. to create results, development, and wellbeing' – Henrik Schelde-Andersen, Asbjørn Molly-Søholm, and Thorkild Molly-Søholm.

On the other hand, coaching can also be a tool which the manager can apply to clarify whether or not the company can offer the employee the development they want. Coaching can in this way unearth the professional's goals, and the manager can then assess whether it will be possible for the employee to engage with the desired areas, and thereby realize their needs for development. Coaching thus becomes a basis on which the manager in concrete terms is able to communicate to the employee whether or not their wishes can be fulfilled in the unit in question, or even in the firm at large. This provides a good platform for the employee to assess their own development needs in the light of their keenness to remain in the firm.

Recognizing the individual

Tailoring management input to the needs of the individual – and to be seen to be doing this – is very important, not least to ensure the necessary credibility to support the professional genuinely in their development. Such credibility is created by being present for the professional, and being ready and willing to discuss issues that matter to them – if appropriate, personally as well as in their working life.

For instance, if a professional is nervous about presenting to large audiences or about how a client will receive a report, the manager should provide support in preparing for the task, later following up on how it went. This will demonstrate that the manager cares and is interested, while providing a forum to discuss onward action if this is needed. Others, however, will respond by asking not to be controlled when it comes to the same type of activity.

Professionals will read more into the manager's actions than their words and promises. It is here that values come to life. Without follow-through, the words will have an empty ring and the manager will lose credibility with the individual. Walk the talk.

Great professionals don't necessarily make great managers

All this adds up to a lot of responsibility on the manager's shoulders. Since professionals are integral to the firm's success, whether the firm operates in the private or public sector, any wrong decision made by leaders could have direct and dire consequences for the business and its clients.

It seems surprising, then, that so many managers in knowledge-intensive firms have been appointed not by virtue of their skills in employee development, but because of their professional competences: they have risen to the top because they have been recognized as the best or most senior lawyer/economist/consultant/accountant/engineer, etc. – or perhaps because of their track record at selling. None of these qualities necessarily makes them any more likely to be an excellent, natural manager and leader of other professionals, however. Without appropriate training, and the right basic skills in the first place, such managers will face significant challenges in retaining good professionals in the long run, for all the reasons discussed throughout this book.

Through our own extensive experience of managing and researching management in knowledge-intensive firms, we have concluded that, in the great majority of cases, knowledge-intensive firms should hire managers who have *people* skills first and foremost, particularly as such skills are difficult to learn if they don't already exist naturally.

It is our impression that managers dedicated to the wellbeing and development of professionals create a strong firm, because a real interest in professionals' needs engenders more loyal, dedicated professionals who feel like taking responsibility and fighting for the cause – characteristics that are difficult to engineer synthetically.

Managers know, just as professionals know, that if you are have a genuine interest in your employees, if you feel empathy, you will wish the best for them. Likewise, fulfilled and happy staff will want the best for their firm. Flemming Bligaard Pedersen, CEO of leading Scandinavian engineering consulting firm Rambøll, offers the following advice to other knowledge-intensive firms seeking to employ new managers:

> Genuine management qualifications mean that you can be *primus inter pares*. It is not necessarily the person who is the best professional who should be the manager. In a knowledge-intensive organization you will be exposed if you do not have genuine management competences. You are only the manager if your employees accept you as such. Otherwise you cannot function.

Professionals who have been 'burnt' by a bad management experience – for example, where a manager has failed to assist them in their professional development – may become 'management averse'. But this situation can be turned around with the appointment of a good leader, turning more cynical professionals into receptive members of a learning and developing organization. A good manager, especially in a knowledge-intensive firm, will focus on the possible rather than the impossible, unleashing professionals' talents and seeing what can rather than what can't be done.

Also in the public sector, management styles are shifting to allow creative talent to thrive. At the Danish Ministry of Foreign Affairs, Peter Høier, Manager of the Competence Center (UMKC), comments:

> In the Foreign Service, personnel management is now taken much more seriously. If you cannot deliver in the HR part of the management job, then you are not a manager in the Ministry of Foreign Affairs. You will not be appointed if your 'only' qualification is professional excellence.

Clearly, managing effectively in a knowledge-intensive firm is difficult and challenging, but it is also fun to lead when you succeed and are able to liberate considerable levels of energy among professionals, because they have benefited from the right dose of responsibility and coaching.

System management vs. daily operational management

Management is a discipline, a way of thinking, and not just something that can be carried out as a series of tasks. Effective management will be exercised in various spaces and with various tools.

As demonstrated throughout this book, management is greater than the sum of all its constituent parts. It reaches beyond the firm's organization and structure, the establishment of a given business model, and the implementation of a number of systems and information technologies. It is defined by the cultural modeling of professionals, who promote your preferences as a manager. This value-based management is vital in knowledge-intensive firms, where the direct actions of professionals and the decisions they take are the primary means by which company strategy is executed.

One way of understanding what this means in practice is to distinguish between *system* management and *daily operational* management as laid out by consultants in Danish Attractor, a management consultancy that is part of the Rambøll Group.

System management is the type of management applied by top executives, executed via formal systems and policies. The remit here is comprehensive and far-reaching across the firm. A lot of written communication may be applied, supported by personal performances in front of all staff at special events, where staff are encouraged to tow the firm line and sing from the same hymn sheet with a view to providing a consistent look and feel, and brand experience, to the outside world.

In such environments (for example, huge global empires), top executives will not have a close, direct relationship with all professionals. Instead, they must focus on ensuring that company systems function and support the company strategy and business model efficiently. Knowledge-sharing systems, concepts for assignment solutions, and approaches to sales may be implemented centrally, aiding consistency and efficiency.

Middle managers will be important lynchpins here, through which top executives seek to generate support for the strategy and preferences of organizational behavior. An important senior management competence therefore will be to be able to create meaningful work for mid-tier managers through an engaging and enthusiastic strategy to liberate energy in the organization and create a shared project.

Daily operational management, in this scenario, becomes the responsibility of mid-level managers who will execute company strategy through interaction with each individual professional. Thus, mid-level managers make the company strategy concrete and interesting – implementing it, defending it, bringing it to life.

Daily operational management is direct management which takes place through the personal contact with professionals. To a great extent, this takes the form of supervision, feedback, mentoring, and coaching of professionals in relation to concrete problems and challenges faced by professionals. As in many other organizations, mid-level managers in knowledge-intensive firms are exponents as well as facilitators of the application of the company strategy on the individual level. This is what we call cultural modeling – the value-based management which instills company values among professionals in a dialog process where managers' and professionals' preferences influence each other in continuous development.

The strategic actions of knowledge-intensive firms are implemented in an interchange between what management aim to do, and what professionals aim to do translating into practice via concrete decisions. The better able the management is to make clear optimal behavior, to ensure value to the firm and to professionals formulating a powerful, sense-making strategy (explaining the rationale of what is chosen to do and not to do), the more effective the execution of strategy will be.

Challenges for top executives will be to support further mid-level managers in their cultural modeling of the organization. The ability to delegate responsibility to middle managers, so that they can take appropriate action in their direct relationships with professionals, is crucial. Thus, middle managers should not just apply the top executive system management approach of communicating profitability, efficiency, costs, time horizons, and so on. This would not motivate professionals as they do not supply their time and commitment to the company to uphold this type of value, but to ensure professional development for themselves and the firm.

Management by market

Examples of various management tasks in knowledge-intensive firms can be found in Table 8.1. As highlighted here, the manager's strategic focus will vary in accordance with the type of market being served, and therefore the business model the firm should apply.

Managers in markets characterized by low customization services must have a consistent focus on the market, and on profit-optimizing initiatives, standardizing the business in order to service the market efficiently. Professionals should naturally also be given attention, but in this market fewer specialized professionals will be recruited.

Managers in markets characterized by higher levels of customization should focus on the clients and their unique challenges, in order to be able to generate creative solutions that match these specific requirements. Professionals here are likely to be creative experts who are capable of challenging the client.

Managers in markets characterized by low client interaction must have a constant focus on the market when it comes to sales. Services and processes must be standardized and optimized. Professionals here will be experts, and their competence profiles must be maintained as such.

Where there is high client interaction, managers will need a consistent focus on professionals' unique competences. In this way, the firm will be able to offer the market individualized services at any time, providing solutions that address the client's unique needs, whether for process support, facilitation, or strategic consulting.

TABLE 8.1 Management tasks vary by market

	Customization		*Client interaction*	
	Low	High	Low	High
Strategic focus	The market (optimization)	The client (the client's challenges)	The market (optimization)	Employees (competences for client handling)
Level of goals	Individual	Team	Team	Firm
Status/reward toward	Optimization Sales	Creativity Solutions	Sales Loyalty	Client satisfaction The client develops
Profiles	Sales people	Creative	Specialists	Facilitators
Recruitment	Younger salespeople	Experts	Experts and younger people	Experienced people
Price	Low	Medium	Low or high (if expert competence)	High
Leverage	High	Medium/high	Medium	Low
Promotions	Efficient Good supervisors	Good at client service	Experts	Those who develop their own client relations
Competition	High	Lower	High	Lower
Competence development	Lower	Medium	Medium	High

Time management

Managers of knowledge-intensive firms face a constant pressure to get involved in more tasks than they can possibly accomplish at a high level of quality. The pressure is caused by many factors, both external and internal.

External factors: when managers are appointed managers because of their strong professionalism, they will remain an important resource for assignments. The manager continues to represent high value in terms of quality and efficient performance on assignments, so clients who are aware of this will continue to ask for the manager to be involved in assignments. As a manager you have a strong client base – that is how you demonstrated success which got you to the management position.

Internal factors: professionals tend to be most excited and inspired by challenging assignments, through which their professional competences are confirmed and enhanced. Being active in assignments also means that they retain and develop their connection to the market and to market trends, while raising their own market value through the acquisition of updated experience. If the manager joins the project team, this too will be appealing as a means of transferring competences and providing feedback to less experienced team members.

In some knowledge-intensive firms, taking on management tasks is seen to have lower status to executing client responsibility and client work. This is to suggest that development and results are created only in the market with clients, and not internally in the knowledge-intensive firm. Consider the surgeon whose scalpel is removed so that they can lead and inspire from an office and teaching space.

Though under huge pressure to stay at the coal-face, it is important for managers to be able to say no and step back, prioritizing management tasks such as developing professionals by motivating, mentoring, giving feedback, and coaching.

Bjarke Ingels, owner of the international architect firm BIG, knows the challenges involved in being a manager who is also involved in production:

> I have a bad conscience about not being sufficiently present and giving the professionals good feedback to develop them. They really miss my commitment in individual projects and that is also where my heart is. That and the client contact. However, since we hired a manager, the situation has already improved a lot.

It is difficult to establish definitively how much time a director should spend on people management compared with client assignments. However, we would assert that managers in knowledge-intensive firms have traditionally neglected and assigned a relatively low level of priority to people and organizational management tasks.

Ideally, this needs to change. It is of much more value to knowledge-intensive firms that the managers contribute to the development and the motivation of professionals rather than produce too much and risk not having time to invest in development. A manager increasing their own billing with 10 percent will not make a significant difference to the bottom line, whereas a manager capable of motivating 10, 20, or 30 professionals to give 10 percent more of themselves – in the number of working hours, efficiency, and/or quality in assignments – will have a significant, tangible impact on the business.

Højer at the Danish Ministry of Foreign Affairs sums it up this way:

> As a manager, your time-horizon is under pressure. Hence your ordinary work is after 4 p.m. when your professionals have gone home. I believe that the main change in management from the past to the present is that these days it just does not do to neglect professionals. Personnel management tasks take up more time, and if you do not take that seriously, they leave and then you really have a problem. So no matter how competent you are professionally, the house of cards will topple if you do not take personnel management seriously.

Summary

Throughout this book we have attempted to make the case that strategy and professionals are equal factors in the creation and management of a successful knowledge-intensive firm.

In this chapter, we have further emphasized that, while professionals in knowledge-intensive firms constitute the primary assets of the business, a firm which opportunistically adapts to the whims and wants of its professionals can have no strategic focus, which is ultimately damaging to the business. Yet, equally, a strategy should not be detached from the needs of professionals, and their competences and preferences. The ideal scenario should see strategy establishing goals and guidelines, while also demonstrating due consideration for the professionals in the firm. Strategic action, meanwhile, is successfully combining the two.

It is an essential management message to private sector as well as public sector knowledge-intensive firms that management should create *meaning* for professionals, motivating and inspiring them in their work. If professionals do not believe that what they do is significant and will make a real difference, they will stagnate. They will fail to deliver optimal quality and may leave the firm.

Mentoring and coaching can help here, releasing competences and energy within the professional in accordance with the firm's interests and strategic focus, while making them feel valued and important.

Given all these substantial challenges and demands on leaders of knowledge-intensive firms, we have gone on to conclude that this demands the recruitment of managers with specific *people* skills, particularly where the remit is daily operational management, working directly above and with coal-face professionals.

Finally, we would like to stress that management demands time – time which cannot be allocated to this vital role as long as managers are still being pulled into live everyday project work. As we have noted, managers aiming to add too much to the bottom line will not have as much impact as managers devoting sufficient time to developing and motivating a larger group of professionals so that they in turn are able to perform better.

Questions for reflection

- Do you know whether your firm's strategy makes good sense to the majority of your professionals?
- Do you and your manager group spend the main part of your time on strategy and the development of professionals, or on billable client assignments?
- Where would you position your firm on a scale from 1 to 10 (where 1 is inferior and 10 superior) in terms of making strategic decisions with equal consideration for the firm's strategy and the preferences of professionals?
- How would you characterize the three main management challenges in your firm?

9
EPILOG

Around 15 years ago, management guru and author David Maister wrote that 'Professional service firms have been managed in one of two ways – badly or not at all!'

Most knowledge-intensive firms are not in such dire straits today, as a number of firms have made improvements in management practice a key focus over the past five to ten years. However, Rome was not built in a day and there remain many opportunities for further progress.

The purpose of this book has been to contribute to the stimulation of management development and the refinement of practices through which knowledge-intensive firms and their managers can reinforce their management performance and capacity.

As we have seen, this is not an easy task, as strong management of a knowledge-intensive firm requires skills and sensitivity across a range of focus areas. This book proposes no miraculous formula for success. Key to achieving tangible improvement will be a lot of hard work, with a practical focus on the critical elements examined over the previous eight chapters.

Encouragingly, plenty of evidence exists to support the finding that where this effort is expended, the resulting good management should fuel a firm's business opportunities, professional quality level, profits, and reputation – all essential ingredients in the development of successful firms and for those outside the commercial sector.

A successful knowledge-intensive firm can only be achieved if clients as well as professionals are nurtured and developed. Aligning the needs of the two requires a clear strategy. Retaining professionals with the right attitude and competences, creating enthusiasm and dedication among these core assets, must be a constant area of focus. If these approaches, as well as quality in client relationships, are maintained over time, the opportunity of creating a successful business is considerable. All experiences confirm this.

It is our impression that many knowledge-intensive firms and their managers – whether in the private, public, or third sector – have understood the management rationale of how such firms should be managed. Yet it is also our view that there is much to be desired in firms' various attempts to achieve 'best management practice'. In many firms, there remains a considerable gulf between intention and practice. If this can be reduced by reinforcing practice and execution, much will be achieved. We hope that this book can act as a practical guide, and provide reassurance and encouragement in the process.

REFERENCES AND BIBLIOGRAPHY

Baschab, J. and Piot, J. (eds) (2005) *The Professional Services Firm Bible*. Hoboken, NJ: Wiley.
Boddy, D. (2005) *Management: An Introduction*. Upper Saddle River, NJ: FT- Prentice Hall.
Czerniawska, F. and Smith, P. (2010) *Buying Professional Services*. London: Economist.
Czerniawska, F. and Toppin, G. (2005) *Business Consulting: A Guide to How it Works and How to Make it Work*. London: The Economist.
Daft, R.L. (2005) *The Leadership Experience*. Mason, OH: Thompson South-Western.
DeLong, T.J., Gabarro, J.J. and Lees, R.J. (2007) *When Professionals Have to Lead. A New Model for High Performance*. Boston, MA: Harvard Business School Press.
DeLong, T.J., Gabarro, J.J. and Lees, R.J. (2008) 'Why mentoring matters in a hypercompetitive world', *Harvard Business Review*. January: 115–21.
DeLong, T.J. and Vijayaraghavan, V. (2003) 'Let's hear it for the B-players', *Harvard Business Review*, June: 96–102.
Drucker, P. (1993) *On the Profession of Management*. Boston, MA: Harvard Business School Press.
Dunn, P. and Baker, R. (2003) *The Firm of the Future – a Guide for Accountants, Lawyers and other Professional Services*. Hoboken, NJ: Wiley.
Edersheim, E.H. (2004) *McKinsey's Marvin Bower. Vision, Leadership and the Creation of Management Consulting*. Hoboken, NJ: Wiley.
Empson, L. (2007) *Managing the Modern Law Firm*. London and New York, NY: Oxford University Press.
George, B. (2007) *True North: Discover your Authentic Leadership*. Hoboken, NJ: Wiley.
Goffee, R. and Jones, G. (2007) 'Leading clever people', *Harvard Business Review*, March: 72–79.
Greiner, L. and Poulfelt, F. (eds). (2009) *Handbook of Management Consulting – the Contemporary Consultant. Insights from World Experts*. London: Routledge.

Hansen, M.T., Nohria, N. and Tierney, T. (1999) 'What's your strategy for managing knowledge', *Harvard Business Review*, March–April: 106–16.

Heskett, J., Sasser, W.E. jr, and Schlesinger, L. (1997) *The Service ProPit Chain*. New York, NY: Free Press.

Hitt, M.A., Bierman, L., Shimizu, K. and Kochhar, R. (2001) 'Direct and moderating effects of human capital on strategy and performance in professional service firms: a resource-based perspective', *Academy of Management Journal*, 44: 13–28.

Holt Larsen, H. (2006) *Human Resource Management – Licence to work*. Holte, Denmark: Valmuen.

Howard, J.H. (1991) 'Leadership, management, and change in the professional service firm', *Business Quarterly*, 55: 111–18.

Jacoby Petersen, N. and Poulfelt, F. (2002) 'Knowledge management in action: a study of knowledge management in management consultancies', in A.F. Buono (red.) *Research on Consulting Series 1*. Greenwich, CT: Information Age Publications.

Kam, W.P. and Singh, A. (2004) 'The pattern of innovation in the knowledge intensive business services sector of Singapore', *Singapore Management Review*, 26: 21–44.

Kim, W.C. and Mauborgne, R. (2005) *Blue Ocean Strategy. How to Create Uncontested Market Space and Make the Competition Irrelevant*. Boston, MA: Harvard Business School Press.

Lorsch, J.W. and Tierney, T.J. (2002) *Aligning the Stars. How to Succeed when Professionals Drive Results*. Boston, MA: Harvard Business School Press.

Lorsch, J.W. and Tierny, T.J. (2009) 'High performance consulting firms', in L. Greiner and Poulfelt, F. (eds) *Handbook of Management Consulting*, London: Routledge.

Løwendahl, B. (2005) *Strategic Management of Professional Service Firms*. Copenhagen: Copenhagen Business School Press.

Maister, D.H. (1993) *Managing the Professional Service Firm*. New York, NY: Free Press.

Maister, D.H. (1997) *True Professionalism. The Courage to Care about your People, your Clients and your Career*. New York, NY: Free Press.

Maister, D.H. (2001) *Practice What You Preach. What Managers must Do to Create a High Achievement Culture*. New York, NY: Free Press.

Maister, D.H., Green, C.H. and Galford, R.M. (2000) *The Trusted Advisor*. New York, NY: Free Press.

Maister, D.H. and McKenna, P.J. (2002) *First Among Equals. How to Manage a Group of Professionals*. New York, NY: Free Press.

Management Consulting Association (2010) *Value of Consulting in Practice*. London: MCA.

Mayson, S. (2007) *Law Firm Strategy. Competitive Advantage and Valuation*. London and New York, NY: Oxford University Press.

McKenna, P.J. (1995) *Herding Cats – a Handbook for Managing Partners and Practice Group Leaders*. The Edge Group.

McKinsey & Company (2001) *War for Talent*, (available online at www.McKinsey.com).

Mikkelsen, M.H. and Poulfelt, F. (2009) 'Getting strategy to work: achieving strategic effectiveness in practice', in T.F. Yeager and P. Sorensen (eds) *Strategic Organization Development*. Greenwich, CT: Information Age Publishing.

Molly-Søholm, A.T. and Andersen, H.S. (2008) 'Leadership-based coaching (Ledelsesbaseret coaching)', *Erhvervspsykologi* 6, May.

Netterstrøm, B. (2002) *Stress på arbejdspladsen* (Stress at Work) (in Danish). Copenhagen: Hans Reitzels Forlag.

Peters, T. (2006) *Re-imagine! Business Excellence in a Disruptive Age*. London: Dorling Kindersley.

Peters, T.J. and Waterman, R.H. Jr (1982) *In Search of Excellence. Lessons from America's Best-run Companies*. New York, NY: HarperCollins.

Ridderstråle, J. and Nordström, K. (2001) *Funky Business*. London: Financial Times/ Prentice Hall.

Robertson, M., Scarbrough, H. and Swan, J. (2003) 'Knowledge creation in professional service firms: institutional effects', *Organization Studies*, 24: 831–57.

Starbuck, W.H. (1992) 'Learning by knowledge-intensive organizations', *Journal of Management Studies*, 2: 713–40.

Storch, J., Sørensen, C., Keiding Pedersen, L., Solsø, K. *Resultatorient-erede medarbejderundersøgelsec* (Results-oriented Employee Surveys), Copenhagen: Lindhardt & Ringhoff.

Sveiby, K.E. and Lloyd, T. (1987) *Managing Know-how – Add Value by Valuing Creativity*. London: Bloomsbury.

Winch, G. and Schneider, E. (1993) 'Managing the knowledge-based organization: the case of architectural practice', *Journal of Management Studies*, 30: 923–36.

Zabala, I., Panadero, G., Gallardo, L.M., Amate, C.M., Sánchez-Galindo, M., Tena, I. *et al.* (2005) 'Corporate reputation in professional services firms: 'reputation management based on intellectual capital management', *Corporate Reputation Review*, 8: 59–71.

INDEX

Accenture 41, 63, 78, 108, 164
Accenture Institute for High Performance Business 164
Accenture Institute for Public Service Value 164
accounting sector 75
advisory services 85
Analysys Mason 50
appraisals (*see also* feedback) 77, 115–16
Arup 27–8, 141
Attractor 175, 178
authentic identity 86

Bain & Company 5, 29, 41, 67
Bech-Bruun 41
BIG 181
billing ratio (*see also* fees) 42
Birds Eye iglo Group (BEiG) 67–8
Bligaard Pedersen, Flemming 20–1, 54, 140–1, 177
bonus 43, 56, 77, 94, 119
Boston Consulting Group 41, 70, 86
Bower, Marvin 144, 187
brand (*see also* identity) xii, 15, 21, 25, 74, 79, 82–3, 87, 96, 99 107–8, 157, 161, 163–4, 178
Brayshaw, Angie 156
Brumwell, Ian 72
Bush, George W. 112

Buscher, Volker 27, 141
business models x, xv, 34, 44–5, 47–8, 51
buying solutions 57

Cahill, Brendan 21, 85
capacity (*see also* resources) 15–16, 21–2, 26, 46, 76, 103, 129, 149, 184
change 10, 12, 23, 48, 66–7, 69–70, 84, 120, 130, 149, 171–2, 183, 188
Cap Gemini 41
client adaptability 8
client development 40, 86, 88, 153
client development strategy 153
client expectations 66, 90–1, 98
client dissatisfaction 36
client interaction 9, 26, 60, 62, 65–6, 68, 70, 75, 79, 87, 180
client satisfaction 5, 28–30, 32–3, 73, 77, 91, 101, 104, 157, 162–3, 179
client selection 137
Colborn, Gordon 55
commodity services 1
concept-based delivery 74
conceptually-based services 74–5
confidence formula 150
cultural modeling 27, 96, 128–9, 131, 133, 135, 137, 139–41, 143, 145–7, 168, 170, 178–9

customized services (*see also* targeted services) 3, 8, 25, 64, 87

Dahl 41
Danish Competition Authority 88 94, 101, 105, 107, 171
Danish State Financial Service Center 157
Department for International Development (DFID) (UK) 45–6
Department for Work and Pensions (DWP) 69–70, 129–30, 156
deviance 142
differentiation 18, 25, 27, 49, 65, 96, 115

Ernst & Young 119
Economic and Social Research Council 46
Elmasry, Hassan 155–6
employee capital 100–1, 103, 105, 107, 109, 111, 113, 115, 117, 119, 121, 123, 125, 127
employee development 77, 105, 115, 175–6
employee satisfaction (*see also* motivation-based management) 29, 115, 146
environment 27–8, 47, 134, 163, 173
Evans-Tranumn, Shelia 56, 112, 171–3
execution xv, 4, 7, 36, 39, 82, 140, 142, 145, 148–9, 151, 153, 155, 157, 159, 161, 163, 165, 179, 185

facilitation 10, 180
farmers 158–9
fees (*see also* billing ratio) xiv, 21, 24, 32, 37–40, 42, 45, 48, 62, 64–5, 68–70, 73, 87, 91, 95–6, 105, 133, 144, 154
feedback (*see also* appraisals) 6–7, 19, 29–30, 102–4, 111, 115, 126–7, 143, 173, 178, 181
fee rates 32, 56, 79
Financial Services Consulting 156
'*Funky Business*' 24, 189

Gartner Group 164
Gersing, Agnete 88, 94, 101, 105, 107, 171

global consulting 41, 78
global firms 8, 63, 70
Goldmann Sachs 94
Gorissen Federspiel 41
growth strategy 74
Grünbaum, Lotte 47, 134, 163
guiding principles xvi, 52, 85, 137

Harper, Julian 21
Harvard Business Review 111, 187–8
Harvard Business School 5, 187–8
Hewitt Associates 66
hit rate 40
holistic management 167, 169, 171, 174, 176, 178, 179, 182
Howarth, Tanya 68
Høier, Peter 47
hunters 158–9

IBM 15, 164
IdeaWatch 164
identity (*see also* brand) xv, 35–6, 62, 82, 86–8, 90, 96, 99
incentive structures 73, 95, 98, 158, 160
Independent Franchise Partners LLP 155
innovation 17, 19, 22, 24, 33, 57, 143, 146, 157, 162, 173, 188
innovative solutions 19–20, 22, 33
Ingels, Bjarke 181
Institute of Development Studies (IDS) 45, 57–8, 136
internal service function xiv, 10
internal service organization xii, xiii
International Profit Associates 97
interplay (*see also* relationships) xv, xvi, 2–3, 13, 128, 148, 167, 170

Jones, Simon 50
junior professionals 106, 117

Kierkegaard, Søren 149
knowledge content 9, 58, 60, 62–3, 68–9, 79
knowledge sharing 3–4, 7, 44, 95, 113, 115, 117–23, 151, 161, 178
KPMG 85, 113–14, 120–1, 160

Index

Kromann Reumert 41–2, 92, 114, 122, 155, 174

Lavesen, Anders 42, 92, 114, 122, 137, 155, 174
leadership xii, 5–6, 13, 47–8, 56, 64, 111, 187–8
Lett 41
leverage 37, 40–3, 60, 63–5, 69, 79–80, 86, 117, 129, 180
lone wolves 79, 141
long-term value 35–6
Lorsch, Jay 5, 101, 188
Lotus Notes 119
Løwendahl, Bente 44, 188

Macken, Graham 156
Maister, David 6, 28–9, 77, 150, 184, 188
Maddison, Elizabeth 46, 57, 109, 136, 188
Management Consultancies Association (MCA) 3
management skills ix, 68
managing expectations 90 96
market 'web' 60–1, 73, 75, 79–80
Masters Kommunikation 88
Matrix Group 66
McKinsey & Company xiv, 41, 107–8, 110, 117, 144–5, 164, 188
McKinsey Quarterly 164
measuring success (*see also* performance management) 18
medical sector 22
mentoring 173, 178, 181, 183, 187
Ministry of Foreign Affairs (DK) 47, 105, 177, 182
Ministry of the Environment (DK) 47, 134, 163
Morgan Stanley Investment Management 155–6
motivation-based management (*see also* employee satisfaction) 173
myths 11, 13

Navigant 155, 156
Netterstrøm, Bo 124–5, 189
New York State Department of Education (NYC DoE) 56, 171
niche strategy 74

Nicholson, David 71–2
Northern Trust 156
Nørretranders, Tor 151

Office of Government Commerce (OGC) 57
'one firm' firms 77–9
operational improvement 21, 85
Ordnance Survey 45, 145
organizational structure xv, 76
outlook 164, 170
ownership 7, 10–11, 84, 140–2

performance appraisal 77, 173
performance management (*see also* measuring success) 57
Perryer, Jaqui 69, 130
Peters, Tom 101, 189
Plesner 41
presence *v.* absence management 101
professional services firm xiii, xiv, 113, 187, 189
profitability xv, 5, 14, 28, 37, 39, 53, 63, 69, 83, 85, 91, 133, 137–8, 162, 171, 179
profitability models xv
profit drivers 27, 34, 37–8, 40, 42, 49, 52, 73, 79, 83
PRTM 55

quality levels 99

Rambøll 20–1, 54, 140–1, 175, 178–9
Rambøll, Børge 140
Rambøll Management Consulting 49–50, 169
RedOwl 22
recruitment xvi, 3, 5, 20, 23, 27, 43, 52, 54, 66, 69, 73–4, 77, 82–3, 86, 90, 95, 98, 107–8, 117, 126, 133, 139, 143, 168, 180, 183
relationships (*see also* interplay) xii, 4, 64, 66–7, 87, 101, 122, 154, 156–61, 165–6, 170, 173, 179, 185
remuneration 5, 39, 65, 83, 104, 119
reputation 5, 15–16, 20, 27, 35–6, 40, 64, 71, 82, 87, 90–2, 108–9, 116, 142, 150, 162, 170, 184, 189

resources (*see also* capacity) 15–16, 21, 26, 28, 36–7, 39–40, 44–5, 48–9, 56, 64–5, 77–80, 87–90, 94, 96, 99, 105–6, 108, 114, 126, 130, 133–4, 137–8, 144–6, 149, 152, 153–4, 157–9, 161, 164–6, 170, 172–3
resource management 133, 188
retention 3, 5, 107–8, 134, 138
return on investment (ROI) 157

SAP 67
Schnedler, Søren 88, 139
service delivery xvi, 3, 29, 44–5, 69, 76
service-level agreements (SLAs) 47–8
service proposition 19
service optimization 25
Siemens 71
standardized services 3, 8–9, 23–5, 63–4
standardized solutions 19, 21–2, 26, 33, 64
Stewart, Andrew 156
strategic action 95, 129, 146, 168, 179, 182
strategic identity xv, 35–6, 62, 82, 87–8, 90, 99
stress 123–6, 189
Sørensen, Carsten 50, 189
support function 9

talent recruitment x
talent wars xiv, 107
targeted services (*see also* customized services) 8, 58
team-based firms 76
team performance 76, 112–13
team-playing skills 76

The Financial Times 155
The Point 164
third sector ix, xii, xiii, 10, 35, 39, 185
thought leader 163–4, 166
thought leadership 64, 163, 165
Tiernan, Tony 86
Tierney, Thomas 5, 101, 188
time management 181
Trinity Horne 21–2, 71–3, 85
Trust 20, 28, 71–2, 141, 149, 152, 154, 156, 160–1, 165–6

UK Treasury 56
'up or out' culture 116–17
utilization 37–40, 49, 79–80, 97

value-based billing 38
value-based management 79, 128, 131, 144, 146, 168, 178–9
value-creating processes 44
value chain vi, 9, 24, 58, 60, 67, 70, 73, 79, 91, 93, 162, 165
value creation 1–3, 5, 7, 9, 11–13, 34–6, 45, 48–9, 79, 138
values contents xvi, 2–4, 6, 12–14, 35, 70, 77, 81, 83, 87, 96, 99–100, 107, 114, 122, 128–33, 135, 137, 139, 140–8, 157, 167–8, 170, 179

Wachtell, Lipton, Rosen & Katz 19–20, 43, 64
Wall Street Journal 155
Watmough, Steve 55, 139
Woods, Tiger 108
World Bank 46

Xantus 55, 67–8, 139